"Elizabeth has succeeded in sharing The Ultimate Experience in Personal Growth. You are about to understand something you have probably never been able to imagine. I have thanked her for what I learned, you will too."
- **Bob Proctor**, author, **You Were Born Rich**

"So often we search for the meaning of life, then we realize that Life is Life... and if we want more it is up to us to create it regardless of what we face. Elizabeth shares how she created more life in the face of her husband's cancer and death."
Mark Shearon author, **Good Grief: Making Sense Out of Death, Dying and Funerals**

"With precise guidance Elizabeth takes you on a real-life journey of intense disillusionment, self reflection and profound inner awakening. A great book for anyone looking for the true meaning of life altering events!"
Andreas Moritz, author, **Freedom from Judgment**

"We can all learn from Elizabeth's raw honesty and heart-felt sharing of her personal journey as the wife of a cancer patient. Take the opportunity to learn how to live every day fully and passionately in the face of challenges."
Tina Shearon, author, **Begin Living Your Life... As You Wish!**

Wednesdays at the
Fluff 'n' Fold

To Lexter –
Bow-wow. Sniff-Sniff
With tail wagging –
Elizabeth
Cahalke

Wednesdays at the Fluff 'n' Fold
A Caregiver's Oasis

The journey called cancer
from a loved one's perspective

Elizabeth Cabalka

Annandale, Minnesota U.S.A

Published by :
Healthy Insights Press
P.O. Box 438
Annandale, MN 55302

Wednesdays at the Fluff 'n' Fold: A Caregiver's Oasis
ISBN:0-9744062-0-1
LCCN:2003110291

Editors: Patricia Dambowy, Cindy Trotto, Barbara Huberty
Illustrations: Patricia Dambowy
Author photographer: Howard Sokol Photography, Denver
Book design: Michael Dambowy and Elizabeth Cabalka
Printer: Bang Printing, Brainerd, MN
First edition. Printed in U.S.A.

For Charles

Howard Sokol Photography, Denver

Elizabeth Cabalka does more than simply philosophize about the topic of caring for a loved one with cancer. She lived the experience. For three and one-half years she and her husband, Charles, lived with cancer. Charles experienced it in his body, Elizabeth experienced it in her soul. She remained by his side through treatments, tests, remission, recurrence and finally death, while striving to learn and grow from the lessons cancer offered.

After nearly a decade in corporate America, Elizabeth founded **Healthy Insights Programs & Seminars.** Since 1995 she has flourished as a business owner, trainer and facilitator, business consultant, and author.

Elizabeth studied foreign language, human potential, and international business in the United States and England. In addition to being a successful business owner Elizabeth is an accomplished musician, sought-after public speaker, stepmother, author, entrepreneur, and lifestyle consultant.

Contents

ACKNOWLEDGEMENTS

ဖ

*"The grateful outreaching of your mind
in thankful praise is a liberation or expenditure
of force; it cannot fail to reach that to
which it is addressed."*
— Wallace D. Wattles,
Author, **The Science of Getting Rich**

ဖ

౭

While this book is about my life, it did not come into being simply through my own efforts. So many people were involved in its creation. This book would still be a compilation of notebook paper, various computer files, and copious stacks of sticky-notes were it not for the efforts and encouragement of countless others. As you hold this book in your hands, know that it bears the marks of many lives.

I have never given birth to a child. If I had I can imagine the feelings of pride, awe and gratitude a parent feels as they hold their baby would be somewhat akin to those I feel as I hold this book. There exists within me a jumble of emotions all tinged with a trace of fear and punctuated by the exclamation, *"Holy cow! What now?"*

I am so very grateful to those individuals who guided the production of this book. Their thorough attention and abundant creativity allowed me to focus on the story as they navigated the myriad of details in the publishing process. My gratitude knows no bounds for their unwavering support and belief in this project.

Without Michael Dambowy, my friend, my partner, and the one who brought color back into my life, this book would not be a reality. His dogged persistence, tireless research and incredible attention to detail were just as invaluable to the project as he is to my life.

For Cindy Trotto, Patricia "Pat" Dambowy and Barbara Huberty, whose hours of editing make me look good, I am humbly grateful. They took my thoughts and writing, often raw and unformed, and polished away the rough edges so the intention of the author and emotion of the journey shine through. In addition to her editing skills, Pat's abundant creativity is showcased in each illustration and the beautiful cover art. What incredible talent she possesses! How grateful I am for her willingness to share it with me.

My love and respect is endless for my brothers and my parents. I am at a loss as to how to adequately express my feelings of appreciation for the sheer joy they bring to my life. Their support throughout my entire life, especially Charles' illness and death, has been unwavering and remains so today. For a richly blessed lifetime filled with tenderness and guidance, they have my deepest thanks.

Charles' family surrounded us in the darkest of times, bringing light and love from the far reaches of the country into our home. I love them and miss our countless hours of Canasta. Christopher, my stepson, I cherish who he has become. He will always be the greatest gift Charles gave to me.

I will be forever grateful to those who walked this road with us: doctors and nurses, colleagues and neighbors, hospice volunteers, church members, ministers and friends. During our most challenging times, Charles and I were uplifted by their presence, refreshed by their support, nourished by the meals they brought, and surrounded by their love.

So many people took the time to read the manuscript in its many forms and shapes. Their feedback and encouragement caused me to write a far better book than I could have written on my own. A very special note of thanks goes to Jill Bishop, my golf partner, mentor, neighbor and friend.

For the skills I acquired and the countless friends I made through my association with PSI Seminars, I am profoundly appreciative. I credit my healing and becoming in large part to them, and I am very proud to be a Women's Leadership Seminar graduate.

Many thanks to Margaret Merrill and her sons, Chris and Ryan. They opened up their New Mexico home to me last winter so I could heal and write. Many pages of this story were written while looking out on the most beautiful place on earth.

I am grateful to the mentors who have richly blessed my life. I have been fortunate to meet and work with many of these fantastic individuals, and some I have not met but simply choose to emulate. Their friendship and teaching has helped me become the person I am today: Ron Buck, Bob Proctor, Andreas Moritz, Dr. John Gray, Mary Manin Morrissy, Mark and Tina Shearon, Dr. Rev. Michael Beckwith, and Larry Wilson.

Many thanks go to my friend and former neighbor, Harvey Mackay. He was the first person to teach me how to be a responsible employee at the ripe old age of twelve. He continues to model my belief that anything is possible.

And to my late husband, Charles, thank you for choosing me nearly ten years ago. Your love still surrounds me and your presence still guides me. This book is for you.

INTRODUCTON

*"To journey without being changed
is to be a Nomad.
To change without journeying
is to be a chameleon.
To journey and be transformed
is to be a pilgrim."*

\- Mark Nepo, author,
The Book of Awakening

❧

By the end of the first day I met him, I knew Charles Winger would change my life. I didn't know that day that we would marry six months later and create a magnificent extended family. Nor did I know I would eventually have the honor of holding him as he lay dying. I simply sensed he would make a profound impact on my life and I would never be the same.

My life was in flux when I met Charles. I was a 30-year-old woman, restlessly seeking the often elusive *"something"*. Exactly what I was seeking I didn't know for sure. I had recently ended a four-year relationship and was once again finding the joy of my own company and freedom. My job, while paying well and keeping me occupied 50+ hours every week, wasn't providing any sort of fulfillment other than the satisfaction of doing it well. My spiritual life was experiencing a perpetual stutter and needed a swift kick in the shorts. While I liked myself for the first time in a long time, something was amiss. I sensed something coming toward me, like a wild animal senses welcome summer rain approaching on the wind.

A few months before we met I left the small but vital church of my youth and joined a large church in downtown Minneapolis. Leaving my small community church was difficult to the point of painful. Yet it was time for me to find a spiritual home of my own.

I had been actively involved in the music program at church for many years, playing flute with a group in a marvelous contemporary worship service. While I loved participating in worship in this way, I realized that I was not truly receiving the spiritual nourishment I so eagerly sought. For example, Holy Communion no longer held the meaning and power it once had for me. I now equated this precious, most holy sacrament to the following:

1. Set flute down.

2. Receive communion quickly in the crowded chancel area and avoid tripping over fellow musicians and ministerial staff.

3. Return to my music stand while clearing my mouth and throat of the host as quickly as possible.

4. Continue playing the appropriate song during the serving of communion. Repeat as necessary until everyone is served.

Not exactly what Jesus had in mind at the last supper I suspect.

It was time for a change so, just as children eventually

leave their childhood home, I left my little church in the suburbs for a big church in the city. This move felt so significant to me that it nearly warranted its own NBC Afternoon Special or perhaps even a theme song.

I was drawn to my new church home for a variety of reasons. The grandeur of the sanctuary, the exceptional music that soared to the rafters, the power of the spoken message and the sheer size of the congregation made for a new and compelling church experience. I also reveled in a sense of relative anonymity after actively participating in the logistics of worship for so many years. I came away from those early Sunday services missing my old friends but feeling more renewed and refreshed than I had in some time.

One Sunday I sat behind a handsome young man with dark hair, a warm smile, a rich singing voice and incredible eyes. I remember shaking his hand with a slightly guilty shudder as the congregation *"passed the peace"*. As I sat down I once again congratulated myself on my fine selection of a new church home. One month later I encountered this gentleman again, not just for a fleeting moment, but for an entire marvelous weekend.

On an unseasonably warm Friday afternoon in March of 1994 I headed out of the city to Koinonia Retreat Center, my new church's hospitality ministry in rural

Minnesota. I had signed up for a *Work & Worship* weekend at this 100-acre haven and was eager to be away from the city for a while. The purpose of the weekend was to provide volunteer labor for a refurbishing project at Koinonia, as well as to bring together congregation members for fellowship and fun. My purpose, however, was very clear although I didn't admit it to anyone else: to meet new people, hopefully of the male persuasion.

I reached my destination by mid-afternoon, long after the other participants arrived and set to work. With the help of a friendly staff member, I found myself in an empty conference room, the site of the weekend's project. My yet unseen colleagues were upstairs enjoying mid-afternoon coffee, conversation and lovingly prepared treats.

The project foreman appeared moments after my arrival and quickly put me to work sanding drywall while perched on a ladder. I worked with great vigor, creating a swirl of white dust that quickly covered my clothing and hair.

A few minutes later the crew returned to work and I was mildly chagrinned to meet my weekend colleagues, whose average age was roughly seventy. I was quickly introduced to a delightful bunch of folks. While I thoroughly enjoy my *"perfectly aged"* friends, I realized immediately that I would have to shift my expectations for the weekend.

After introductions it was back to work I went. Once again I was soon surrounded by an impressive cloud of dust and lost in my work. A short time later a welcome, yet admittedly disturbing, sight caught my eye. Apparently not all my co-workers were of the senior persuasion after all. Six-feet tall, dark hair and beard, piercing eyes and an astonished look to match my own. There he was! The man who passed the peace!

On the outside I was cool and calm, at least as cool as I could be sanding drywall from the fourth rung of a yellow metal ladder. Inside, however, I was completely a wreck and had to remind myself to breathe. I became acutely aware of my ratty old sneakers, my faded jeans with many holes, my pitted-out old turtleneck, and a serious lack of make up. Not to mention, the layer of drywall dust thoroughly whitening my long wavy hair. I later learned that none of this even registered with this intriguing man. As the story goes, he took one look at me and dreamily asked his friend, *"Where did she come from? She's absolutely beautiful."*

A short while later (though it seemed like ages) he came over to introduce himself. *"My name's Charles Winger. What's yours?"* he inquired.

I jumped down off my ladder and thrust out my hand. *"Elizabeth Cabalka. Pleased to meet you. Guess I should get back to work,"* I said in the course of three seconds. Then back up my ladder I scurried to my elevated roost of safety.

Later that afternoon the two of us began a conversation around the open-air fire where some folks were simmering sap for delicious homemade maple syrup. That conversation lasted for the better part of three days. While I was absolutely scared silly, I was drawn to him just as he was drawn to me. When I wanted to run away, he stood his ground and gently drew me back.

We learned quite a lot about each other that weekend. The thing I remember impressing me most about Charles was his commitment to service and his love of life and others. Perhaps it was those very qualities that caused me to fall in love with him.

Charles quickly learned something about me as well. I have always felt that absolutely anything was possible. I was somehow blessed with an absolute assurance that there was nothing I couldn't do. I think perhaps this stems from a congenital hip condition for which, at the ripe old age of 11 months, I had my first of many surgeries followed by nearly 20 months in body casts from the waist down. As a direct result I wore much-hated corrective shoes as a child and walked with a unique gait.

I don't recall being particularly troubled by these things (except the corrective shoes of course), just fiercely determined to be normal like my friends. When anyone said to me, *"You can't do that,"* my response was invariably, *"Oh yeah? Just watch me."*

Charles pointed this out to me that first weekend as we worked on the construction project together. He freely praised my desire to take on things that were new and challenging. At the same time, he commented on my seeming inability to receive support of any kind, though freely given and readily available. How interesting that this comment proved so accurate a few years down the road when I needed support more than ever before. Charles' observation identified what was to become my greatest area of personal growth, as the chapters that follow make abundantly clear.

During the course of our many conversations that first weekend together, we realized we had been in the same place at the same time on numerous occasions many years before. While his career was beginning in Fargo, I was attending college just across the river in Moorhead. We recalled at least a half-dozen times when we had been at the same party or event, yet our paths didn't cross until that day at Koinonia ten years later. Fate? Perhaps. Divine order? I am absolutely certain.

We were married six months after we met in the sanctuary where we first shook hands. While our family and friends were somewhat stunned, frankly so were we. In the midst of it all, however, we both knew that it was meant to be. The few times I became angst-ridden and doubtful during our brief engagement, a gentle pulse or mantra would whisper in my heart. *"Don't waste time,"* it said. *" Don't waste time. You two have important work to do, so just listen to your heart. You are not alone. Don't waste time."* I didn't know how true that was. I simply chose to listen.

A few years later I left my corporate position. While starting my own business, Charles worked at the large downtown church where we first met. Early one summer afternoon Charles called me on my cell phone to ask, *"What would you think about moving to Koinonia?"* the smile apparent in his voice. *"I was just offered the business manager position and there's a place on site for us to live, at least for a little while."*

During that ten-minute conversation we decided to uproot our lives and move out of the city. No dramatics. No pain. Just a simple decision that seemed absolutely right. Once again, everyone around us was a bit baffled to hear the news, yet we both knew it was right for the course of our lives. Turns out we were right. Very, very right.

We didn't simply live at Koinonia for a little while. We lived there for six years. Charles eventually died there. His ashes rest on the many wooded trails and our lives are woven into the fabric of every inch of the place. Even today you can sit near the Serenity Pond on a handsome granite bench that bears his name.

When Charles entered my life, he brought with him a precious little blessing: his son, Christopher. The first time I met him he barely reached past my waist. Yet his blonde hair and sweet second grade smile reached inside my heart and grabbed hold. Now, at age 17, he towers over me and speaks with a deep voice of adolescence. His appearance has changed dramatically, yet his smile still reaches deep into my heart and gives it quite a tug.

One thing that made step-parenting easier was that Charles and Christopher's mother, Cheryl, always seemed to get along. Despite their divorce, they always treated each other with respect, which paved the way for all of us to create a positive working relationship and a comfortable mingling of families. When Charles was diagnosed with cancer, Cheryl quickly became one of my greatest sources of support and friendship. At Charles' funeral, she and I sat beside Christopher, one on either side, creating a warm protective fortress for each other and for him.

Charles and I were married seven years. In that time we experienced happiness and sorrow, tenderness and anger, travel and simplicity, flush times and lean. While our years together seemed short and far too few, they were rich and full of love. We loved completely and then let go.

The process of letting go of a loved one is a painful yet accurate analogy for life. Clinging is easy. Letting go is enormously difficult. Letting go for me required bravery that, despite my deeply rooted self-determination, I didn't know I possessed. Through Charles' illness, we moved from one to the other: first clinging tightly and then letting go, only to grasp and cling again. A nearly imperceptible dance back and forth, back and forth...

Throughout our marriage we both maintained our own separate interests, but our lives were inextricably intertwined as well. Sorting through the many chords that bound us, one to the other, and extracting myself to stand alone began in earnest when it became apparent that Charles was dying.

Who was I with Charles? I was a wife, a partner, a friend and confidant, a stepmother, and one-half of a married couple. Who was I without Charles? This was a question whose answer was unknowable until after he was gone.

In the final months of his life, we both took on a tenderly resolved manner that comes from knowing it would end. We knew we would be parting but didn't want it to be. All the desire to make it otherwise, however, didn't have the power to change the outcome.

In the end we strove to do what was necessary to part in a gentle way, hopefully with some grace and a sense of completion as well. Our communication took on a new clarity and meaning that occasionally included words.

I was right that day I first met Charles. He did change my life irrevocably and forever. While I wouldn't have chosen this particular path of change, I would never trade all I've learned along the way. There is sadness in this story, to be sure. Yet there is beauty here as well. My wish for you is that the beauty in your life is readily evident, not a stranger but an ever present friend.

Chapter One

OUT OF ORDER

*"Praise and blame, gain and loss, pleasure and sorrow come
and go like the wind. To be happy, rest like a great tree in
the midst of them all."*
- Buddha's Little Instruction Book

ℒ

In 1998, my husband, Charles, experienced an immaculate infection that changed our lives forever. Let me explain...

Memorial Day weekend Charles and I went for a long walk on the property of the 100-acre wooded retreat center where we lived. Everything was green, vibrant and alive like a spring day right out of a Minnesota travel brochure.

Later that night, Charles' legs started to itch. A few isolated patches at first, entirely covering his legs one week later. Yessireee! Poison ivy in all its glory. Honestly, to this day I don't know where it came from.

I am a native Minnesotan. As such, I was trained at a very early age to spot and avoid the shiny, three-leafed plant at all cost. During our entire walk, I do not recall seeing even a single shiny leaf that brought to us Charles' immaculate infection.

Seeing the red and growing welts, I knew his condition would get worse before it got better. I watched helplessly as my beloved nearly went mad from the itching and scratching. Despite his misery, it took seven long days before he would agree to see a doctor.

A young Physician's Assistant was on duty at our small-town local clinic that day. He was polite and thorough, blessedly thorough we later discovered.

During the course of Charles' exam the doctor asked, *"Other than 'itchy', how is your overall health? Any complaints or concerns?"*

"I've been having a little trouble swallowing in recent months," Charles admitted. *"It takes more and more liquid to wash down each meal."*

"It's probably nothing, but I'm scheduling a chest x-ray for you tomorrow at Buffalo hospital," he said in his matter-of-fact way.

Charles went for an x-ray the next morning at 9:00 a.m. Quick and painless. In and out in a jiffy. Late that afternoon we received a call saying there was a ten centimeter mass in Charles' esophagus, probably cancerous. As a result, our doctor scheduled an appointment for the next day at another hospital eighty miles away.

At 6:00 a.m. the following morning Charles underwent an endoscopy (a diagnostic test that looks into the throat and stomach) that revealed what we feared most. The doctor who performed the test told us he was certain Charles had stage-three esophageal cancer. He presented us with a full-color photo of the tumor (from four different angles) and sent us on our not-so-merry way.

That was the first time Charles and I heard the word adeno-carcinoma. I'll never forget it. It was as though God had hung a huge *out-of-order* sign around his neck. In an instant, everything became odd and surreal. Hours later we walked through a grocery store realizing that no one knew what was happening in our lives. No one understood how our world had been rocked to the core. To the outside world, we were simply another couple pushing a purple cart through Rainbow Foods. This awareness ignited a spark of curiosity and a deeper compassion for those around me.

In a split second everything changed. It was like slipping into another dimension, but not entirely; or moving through air that had somehow become more dense. At times it was as though I was peering out from within a hard outer shell that happened to look just like me. Unexpected moments were painfully ironic, some to the point of being downright humorous.

For example, a few days after Charles' diagnosis we asked a local surgeon about Charles' chances if he didn't have a massive surgery to address this challenge. *"Well, I wouldn't renew any magazine subscriptions"* was his flippant response.

Charles and I initially found his response somewhat humorous, until we looked underneath that response for the truth of the matter. This was our first experience of the wide range of emotions that would co-exist throughout the entire journey and beyond.

I am grateful every day for the immaculate infection, for it was the prelude to a remarkable chapter in our lives. It also marked the beginning of three and one-half years of intentional living often undiscovered or unknowable without catastrophic events such as these.

So began this chapter of our lives, our journey with the big C. That's right, **OUR** journey. This book is not about my husband's journey. Not directly, although you will get to know him well in these pages. This book is about my journey, his wife, partner, confidant and best friend. Cancer from **my** perspective.

Needless to say, this journey had moments of profound sadness and excruciating, mind-numbing emotional pain. In addition, the journey has provided incredible awareness. I have experienced unfathomable growth and personal discovery to last 100 lifetimes, along with amazing irony and even moments of humor.

Nearly everyone experiencing the journey called *"cancer"* has someone there beside them experiencing the journey in his or her unique way. My journey, and that of other partners of cancer patients, is just as unique, just as important, just as devastating, just as challenging, just as transforming, just as painful, and just as real as that of our partners. Yet, our stories are not often told. They need to be told.

A few weeks after Charles' diagnosis, a friend told me that this chapter in my life-journey was not about me and I was selfish to think I was any part of it. She advised me to forget about myself and told me my role was to be a selfless, silent servant. She criticized our choices of non-traditional medical care and accused me of using Charles as a lab-rat and test case to promote my beliefs in complementary care. These words were hard to hear, yet they caused me to think.

To be sure, this journey has taught me to step outside myself. It taught me patience, the joy of service, and the gift of willingly putting my loved one's needs ahead of my own. I consider these lessons beautiful gifts and treasure them greatly. I have also learned that I matter too. My challenges don't show up on an x-ray or a lab chart, but they are equally real. Charles had his path and I had mine. Both paths had challenges, different as they appeared.

The purpose of this book is to share with you **my** story, that of a partner and caregiver to a cancer patient. I promise it is not unique. I see myself in the faces of countless others nearly every day. Perhaps you will see yourself within these pages as well. It is also possible you will simply find greater compassion for someone you know who is traveling a similar path.

Some of the things I remembered and discovered while writing this book were painful. I chose to look honestly at Charles, our marriage, our beliefs, and our choices. While I uncovered some beautiful memories, the process of self-examination was not always enjoyable. Simply look into a magnifying mirror designed to show every pore and blemish and you will understand. While very effective, it isn't always pleasant. Often more revealing than is comfortable. Yet I chose to look closely and learn from it all.

Are you caring for a loved one with cancer? Are you facing the reality of your wedding vows? Particularly *"in sickness and in health, until we are parted by death"?* Are you frightened and wondering if you are up to the task? I invite you to embrace this experience. Be vulnerable and open to all that lies ahead. Will there be pain? Quite possibly. Yet pain free living is highly over-rated and unrealistic. It is the pain, in fact, that provides an appreciation for peace, joy and rest.

If you are a partner of someone experiencing cancer, I am here to tell you that your journey matters too. You are not alone. This chapter in your life possesses its own inner beauty and the ability make you stronger. I invite you to let it teach you, inspire and transform you.

My prayer is that these reflections touch, entertain, challenge and transform you just as my journey has done for me.

Chapter Two

SORTING

"Don't worry what people may think about you
because most people don't..."
- Charles M. Winger, 1958-2001
Husband, father, brother,
son and friend

❧

In the days following Charles' diagnosis, we were bombarded with enormous amounts of information. Word spread quickly among our friends and colleagues and everyone seemed to want to help. We heard about scores of *little known sure-fire cures for cancer*. Everyone knew someone, who knew someone, who had a sister or cousin or aunt who used some stuff from the bark of the Himalayan *"whatzit"* tree and miraculously got better. The Internet alone provided dizzying amounts of facts and figures, all of them sobering.

And so we began to sort.

Our sorting process was not nearly as simple as colors, whites and towels, but possessed some similar nuances nonetheless, with subtle nagging questions running through the mix. As with laundry there were pressing issues pertaining to *"not quite"* whites, washable silks and questionable hand-washables. In our case questions of quality of life as well as longevity were the issues at hand. These areas are easy to discuss in theory, much more challenging to weigh within the confines of your family.

We initially turned to traditional medicine as our first source of help. At first it seemed straightforward, if not palatable, as we began researching possible treatment options. Within two weeks of Charles' initial diagnosis we made trips to four Minnesota hospitals, including the globally-esteemed Mayo Clinic, (a place one elderly friend referred to as *"Mayos"*, as though it were some trendy new sandwich spread, and this always made us smile).

We talked with countless nurses, five different surgeons, three oncologists and two radiologists. With differing emphasis on the most beneficial element, the pieces were the same: surgery, radiation and chemo-therapy. One surgeon acerbically referred to this plan as the *"slash, burn, and poison"* routine. Charles made an interesting observation while driving home from Mayo clinic. This was the same regimen proposed to his mother as she sought a cure for her brain tumor... twenty-five years earlier. She passed away when Charles was fifteen years old.

In preparation for our appointments, we made up a long sheet of questions to ensure consistency of data gathering and to maximize each visit. We took copious notes and even recorded each session on a hand-held recorder after promising each doctor we would use it only for our own private purposes.

One question we asked everyone was, *"If you were in our shoes, what would you do?"* We found it not at all surprising that the oncologists all recommended plans that heavily favored chemo, the radiologists professed better odds with radiation-heavy regimens, and most surgeons emphatically preached the importance of surgery. With no disrespect intended, is this perhaps why they call it a medical *opinion?*

What was surprising to us was that recommendations about nutrition and lifestyle came from one doctor only. One day he said casually, *"Nutrition's not important."* As an afterthought he added, *"Then again you may want to consider a good multi-vitamin."* From everything we read and learned, diet and lifestyle were directly to blame for creating the problem. We started to ponder whether it could assist in the cure?

After our many appointments we finally arrived home. Our heads were positively swimming with disconcerting medical information. Most sobering, however, was that most research we found coming from the traditional medical path detailed a rigorous, painful and invasive regime whose projected five-year survival rate was seven percent. Yes, seven percent.

In the midst of all this gloom, we were blessed with an angel. Charles' oncologist at our local hospital is quite possibly one of the nicest men on the face of planet Earth. He was clearly an advocate for us as we navigated the winding road of managed care. For three and one half years he treated us with utmost dignity and unwavering respect, even when we made choices that were outside the bounds of what he recommended. While he was Charles' doctor, he became our trusted counselor and valued friend.

A few weeks after his initial diagnosis, Charles began his medical treatment on a traditional path. Five days of hospitalization for intense non-stop chemo therapy left him exhausted, disoriented, nauseous and in great pain. For nearly eight days the sores in his mouth alone made it impossible for him to swallow anything, even his own spit. While we were reassured this was *"normal"*, we quickly realized that we would lose him to it if we didn't try something new.

What nagged at us both was that this was only the beginning. Charles was scheduled to repeat this process four or five more times and undergo a full course of radiation as well. All this would be followed by a massively-invasive surgery to remove nearly his entire esophagus and part of his stomach. The words we often heard were, *"You're a big strong guy, Charles. If we really blast away at you, I think you can take it."*

41

About this time we started asking a different set of questions. Previously we asked ourselves, *"How can we kill the cancer without killing Charles?"* Needless to say, all the talk of killing weighed heavily on our hearts. Coming out of a growing appreciation for the marvelous human body and its propensity to heal itself, our questions soon became, *"How can we assist and support Charles' body to move toward total healing and vital long life?"*

We began to sort all over again.

Sorting became for us like tuning in a radio, or trying on clothing to find what feels good and fits your style. We had great respect for our traditional doctors, yet we felt so compelled to open our thinking to additional options. The stakes seemed too high to look only at a few. We were not closing doors, rather opening them all and a few windows too. We now understood the personal nature of each patient's choice. What would be right for us would not necessarily be right for others. We knew without a doubt that the reverse was true as well.

So many in our life were inquisitive and respectful, as well as supportive and helpful. There were a few however, who were quick to judge, and the vehemence with which they expressed their opinions took us both by surprise. In the face of judgment, Charles would invariably say, *"Don't worry what people may think about you because most people don't..."* He repeated this so often it was quoted at his funeral. With that in mind we continued to sort.

A series of phone calls and a chance meeting with a friend led us to consider a three-week treatment in Mexico. We heard all the horror stories and were initially quite skeptical. At first we even sighed and rolled our eyes. Something just kept gnawing at us to look a little closer. That was our first experience of working with the greatest sorting tool, our own inner nudging.

We made countless phone calls to Mexico and to patients around the continent. We sent scores of e-mails, numerous letters and prayed like warriors. After all that effort, the only thing that was absolutely clear was that we needed to go to Mexico and check it all out. *"It is not clear now but we'll know when we need to know"*, was our favorite phrase and mantra.

On August 28, we boarded a plane to San Diego for more research and a week of vacation. We decided we would both stay in Mexico for his treatment if we felt it would be beneficial. If not, we would return to Minnesota and Charles would undergo surgery at the Mayo Clinic to remove his esophagus.

Not knowing how long we would be away, one week or a month, made packing and preparing an interesting event. In fact, the airlines were threatening to strike the day after we left home. So the question became not only *when* would we come home but also *how?*

We had a wonderful time in San Diego. Our charming hotel was located in the heart of the Gas Lamp District with views of countless restaurants, the sparkling bay, and Coronado Bay Bridge. Having no car, we took trams and trolleys to all points of interest and reveled in new sights and sounds, smells and ideas. For a few days we pretended everything was all right and we were just on vacation. Our trip into Mexico loomed before us, though, casting a shadow over every sun-drenched activity.

The day finally arrived. We crossed the border into another world, our eyes big and round. Our driver drove the narrow crowded roadways at top speed, as though he would be paid by velocity and not distance. We toured two facilities, met with doctors and patients, paying close attention to equipment and remedies as well as how we reacted and how we felt inside.

After a long hot day on the road, we ended up back in the U.S.A. at the Denny's restaurant right near our hotel. Still unclear about our course of action, we flipped over our placemats and individually wrote out all the pros and cons. Our pens scratched for a good long time and our meals went untouched. After we finished, we silently exchanged placemats and read what we saw. They were nearly identical and it was finally clear. We would go to Mexico where Charles would undergo a round of *"alternative"* treatment. Just as we expected, we knew the course of action we should take exactly when we needed to know. Not a moment before.

Charles had remarkable results, at least for a while. Follow up tests a few months later were unable to detect any cancer at all. For over a year Charles was strong and robust. He quickly gained back all the weight he lost and resumed his life.

A routine follow-up visit here at home fifteen months later brought us the news we feared most. The cancer was back and there was nothing traditional medicine could do. Another trip to Mayo Clinic revealed that surgery was no longer a viable option due to the radiation scar tissue along his throat. We vetoed more chemo because of the questionable results. He already had a full course of radiation, so that option was out as well. We respectfully but firmly closed the traditional treatment door.

The path we traveled before was right at the time, but clearly not a path we would travel again. Once again we sorted through all we knew and felt, hoping to find an answer, one that would best fit Charles' needs and hopefully produce a desired outcome.

We attended an extraordinary weeklong teaching seminar with a group in South Dakota. We studied topics such as pH, alkalinity, nutrition and hydration. We read about the digestive process and the importance of our diet. We participated in Qi Gong and various workshops on energy or *"Chi"*. Firmly grabbing our attention was a discussion about the power of the mind. We were both fascinated by books and materials suggesting that the body takes its commands from our thinking, therefore the age-old saying, *"to think is to create."* Charles grabbed on to this philosophy and programmed his thinking for healing and vitality.

We saw patients around us constantly talking about their illness, feeling down and not getting well. We chose differently and focused all our energy on health, vitality and being well. We ate a tasty organic diet, drank gallons of quality filtered water and searched for the blessing in everything to maintain a positive outlook. As a result, Charles experienced seven months of vitality and health beyond anything he had ever experienced in his life. We vacationed every month for the next six months. We took hundreds of photos, made countless memories and collected precious souvenirs.

Then one day I watched as Charles stood up from his chair. He had been experiencing a cold and his coughing was a persistent loud staccato bark. He winced with pain as he stood and softly moaned unaware I was close by. I froze in my tracks, barely breathing, and he finally noticed me. He met my gaze and I saw fear clearly written on his face. Outwardly we pondered pulled muscles or a shoveling injury to his back. Deep within we both knew that something more had changed.

The pain in his back never went away nor did he ever fully recover from that bothersome cold. When a chiropractor suggested he have a doctor take a close look at his pancreas, fear took over Charles' mind and he started to despair. We were told early on, you see, that his type of cancer would most likely spread to the pancreas if it would spread at all. Sadly, the survival stats for pancreatic cancer are even more abysmal than those we already faced.

After a few more months of severe back pain and an additional loss of twenty pounds, his doctor recommended hospice care and we sorted yet again. What did hospice mean to us? The beginning of the end.

At every turn along this path we sorted through it all. Sometimes we did it out loud in a methodical organized way. Most often though we sorted in the privacy of our thoughts, searching deep within for certainty, a message or a sign. Our answers often came not in a document or file, but rather in our feelings or the quiet place of prayer. We made hundreds of important and seemingly trivial choices, and became different people along the way. Our choices reflected who we were at any given moment in time.

While I think of Charles daily, there are no regrets today. I occasionally find myself pondering the *"what ifs"*, but not very often. I found this kind of thinking leads to heartache and emotional ruin. Since Charles passed away, I have sorted through so many thoughts, and found a bit of comfort: I know we did the best we could with the information that we had. And that is enough.

Chapter Three

WEDNESDAYS AT THE
FLUFF 'N' FOLD

*"The greater part of our happiness or misery depends
on our disposition and not our circumstances."*
\- Martha Washington
1731-1802, Former First Lady

૭

A household with cancer is not a *normal* household. (If there is such a thing.) Life changes completely at the moment of diagnosis. Then again, there are parts of life that remain exactly the same. The trash must still go out with regularity to avoid malodorous household experiences. The dishes still collect in the sink. Pets still need to be fed. Groceries must still be bought and put away. Report cards and permission slips must still be signed and returned to school. Dinner must still be cooked, and the laundry must still be washed.

Normal as they are, these things suddenly possess a constant new presence that can make them foreign or absurd. Yet there is something comforting in their mundaneness. There is a reminder of a simpler life, of *before* and *normal*, and a glimmer of hope for simplicity's return.

I found comfort somewhat elusive in the first year of this journey. One place, however, where I regularly found great comfort was the local laundromat. Life at the Fluff 'n' Fold was generally warm, soft, clean, and neatly folded. In the midst of chaos, this was an enormous solace.

The first time I heard the word adeno-carcinoma, my life was unceremoniously dumped into the Spin Cycle and turned on high. I felt as though someone had hurled me into the industrial large load machine, popped in a roll of quarters and walked away.

Amidst the chaos in my mind and soul, the Fluff 'n' Fold became my oasis, a place of comfort and renewal. Each Wednesday I'd pack up my baskets, lug them to the car, drive to town, carry the baskets inside and fill the machines, fumble with quarters, and let the powerful Spin Masters take control. I would lose myself to the process all the while delighting in the sameness. I could convince myself, even for just a little while, that something as challenging as cancer couldn't possibly exist in a place like the Fluff 'n' Fold.

Ask anyone who frequents the laundromat with any regularity, they'll tell you that life's greatest lessons can be discovered within the walls of the Fluff 'n' Fold. Lessons such as:

1. There is no such thing as pride as you wash and fold your whites in a large room with others.

2. The most effective machines are often decorated with out-of-order signs.

3. Comfort comes in odd forms, like standing with your back to a warm jumbo dryer on a cold January day.

Wednesdays at the Fluff 'n' Fold were simple, unlike life in my home. There were rules and a process, orderly outcomes and silent camaraderie, even laundry etiquette was clearly posted on the wall. Everything made sense. The Fluff 'n' Fold was my solace. Its walls became my fortress of escape. For two precious hours every week, I could pretend that everything was just fine.

I invite you to find your oasis as you travel along this road. Find a place that provides peace and order amidst the chaos. On this path these spots are often cleverly disguised and even maddeningly elusive, but without a doubt they are there.

As you seek your oasis, first shift your thinking about what it may look like. Open yourself to the possibility that it may not look at all as you expect. Don't worry about the package it comes in; rather, seek out the feeling. In an experience that can batter the emotions, tune in to the balm and peace that is around and within you, always available.

Chapter Four

THE CHANGE MACHINE

"It is not the strongest of the species that survive, nor the most intelligent, but the one most responsive to change."
\- Charles Darwin
1809-1882, British Scientist

૭૦

The change machine... Bills in. Quarters out. Simple, right? While waiting for my laundry to dry one Wednesday afternoon, I sat writing in my journal. I had reached a crossroads, feeling the need to express something but not knowing what it was. As I looked across a bank of Whirlpool's finest, my eyes rested on the change machine. I had found my inspiration.

How many times had I inserted a dollar bill and thought nothing of the fact that what returned to me were four shiny round quarters? A modern miracle if you ask me. Yet it went unnoticed and unappreciated until that very moment.

Cancer is a change machine like no other. You may go into the experience crisp and neatly folded or perhaps crumpled, limp and slightly torn. The potential exists, however, to come out transformed and shining, all of your value intact, yet somehow more beautiful, somehow more durable, broken down but still shining.

Cancer changes the patient who experiences it in their body as well as the caregiver, whether you want it to or not. The trajectory of my life changed dramatically when Charles was diagnosed with esophageal cancer.

In some ways my life is now unrecognizable, yet my value is still intact. While at times I felt broken down, today I feel more durable, more beautiful and shining. Changed.

I once heard it said that the only one who likes change is a wet baby. I think perhaps that is true. Yet change is a constant. Change is what we can count on. As I look at my life, like those hokey diet ads showing *"then and now"*, I see a myriad of changes that sprouted on this path.

- I am much more comfortable with silence due to the long hours of quiet in my home during the final months of Charles' life.

- I have a greater understanding of what really matters in my life, and I am far more secure in my priorities.

- I am more willing to listen and do not need to fix someone. So many empty platitudes about *"time healing all"*, or *"Charles being in a better place"*, *"It's God's will"*, etc. taught me the value of simply listening.

- I am far more aware of the consequences of my choices regarding what I think, do, eat and say. At the same time, I am equally aware that it serves no greater good to obsess about these things.

- I am abundantly aware of the direct correlation

between diet, lifestyle, and disease.

- I am more aware of what it means to love *"until we are parted by death"*, about loving unselfishly and loving completely.

- I understand the importance of self-care when caring for another.

- I have a deeper awareness of how everything simply *"is"*. We can make it whatever we want. Everyone, patient or caregiver, has their own experience of life. I must allow them to have it without changing or controlling the experience or them.

- I am aware of the unfathomable strength of the human spirit.

- I am aware of the gift of unconditional love, given and received, and the healing balm that it can be to lives in crisis.

Change is often feared because of the inherent element of the unknown. Most people are creatures of habit, myself included, living life on autopilot. For example, we have conversations today that we've had yesterday and may have again tomorrow. We can drive our car across town or cross-country and arrive at our destination marveling at the fact that we don't recall much of the drive. We have Monday meetings, Friday outfits, must see TV nights, a rotating meal plan, speed-dial, etc. Autopilot can serve us well but it can also create a dull, passionless, cookie-cutter life.

What would happen if we lived consciously? What would happen if we really took the time to listen to the voice inside and consciously choose our lives, rather than simply numbing ourselves into a passive prison of circumstance or programmed response?

When Charles was diagnosed with cancer, we began to choose everything consciously. Our arguments became fewer and fewer, yet in some ways more intense as we rediscovered a passion for life and the stakes became significantly higher.

We consciously researched all our options, made different choices about how we spent our time. We were quick to forgive one another and we spent less time in angry silence. We made different choices about the food we ate, our financial matters, our daily exercise programs, and the quality of our time spent with Charles' son, Christopher. We turned off the autopilot and made conscious choices.

Forgive me if I make this sound easy. It wasn't. It is so much easier to simply go with the flow, to be numb and in a rut than to consciously choose life in each moment of each day. Yet, there was a distinct feeling of being fully alive when we stepped out of the rut and firmly grasped the wheel. As you can imagine, I was unable to do this all the time. There were times that reality was so cold and so sharp that I took great care to numb myself completely instead.

Cancer also changed our family. Charles' family, scattered for some time, came together more during Charles' illness than in the preceding 20 years. My family, with our regular rituals, took a look at things differently, creating holiday experiences that were meaningful, not simply dutiful.

At his memorial service one gentleman said, *"Two of the greatest gifts in life are love and death. Sadly, we often pass these gifts on unopened. Not Charles. He shared with us his love. He shared with us his death."*

In the past we were private people. Now we invited people into our lives. We wrote letters, sent out e-mails, and were featured in the local paper. We spoke to groups about our experience, we talked to others from all over the world that were newly facing cancer, and we shared our story to offer hope and perhaps encouragement.

Charles' life touched so many people. So did his death. I received the annual allotment of standard Christmas letters the year he died. In more than one I found the following words, *"this fall I was privileged to share in the life and death of a very dear friend. I learned so much. The experience touched my life. "*

I am changed. Cancer changed me without ever entering my body. Yet, I am grateful for the changes. Not the loss of Charles, but the changes that resulted.

When I entered this experience, I was crumpled, limp and slightly torn. Yet here I am today a little rough around the edges, but transformed and shining. All of my value is intact, yet I am somehow more durable, broken down but shining.

As you travel this path, I invite you to be awake and open to it all. Allow the experience to touch you, to reach inside and mold you. Let it polish away the rough edges so you can fully shine.

Chapter Five

FOLDING

"God leads me beside the still waters
and restores my soul."
- Psalms 23

છ

One simple blessing each Wednesday at the Fluff 'n' Fold was the process of folding. The exercise of folding, stacking, sorting into neat crisp piles was rhythmic and comforting, allowing me to create the illusion of order in my chaotic life.

After extracting my warm, clean treasures from the clutches of the Spin Dry and depositing them into my trusty four-wheeled (sometimes wobbly) laundry chariot, I'd make my way to my work table and begin the process of making sense and creating order. Pressing creases into a pair of jeans, lining up the hems, and gently folding them into a neat little bundle was enormously satisfying. The warmth of the fabric seeped into my hands, then into my heart, where it was often cold and desolate.

Despite a small amount of inevitable frustration produced by matching socks, the predictable process of folding was like a mantra for my soul. In this simple process I found peace. While this peace was temporary, it was peace nonetheless. Creating neat precise stacks, arranged by color, became medicine for my inner being so taxed with colossal burdens and chaos.

I often reflected on how these simple pleasures differed so dramatically from my high profile corporate career of years past. How odd that the simple act of folding clothing had become my greatest satisfaction, replacing pay raises, meetings in boardrooms, tailored suits, and my name on an office door. Those things were part of a lifetime long gone, like a book or story of another person's life. The Fluff 'n' Fold was my oasis in the storm and a microcosm of all that my life had become.

I also found a miniscule amount of control in other simple tasks such as mowing the lawn in precision rows and patterns; cleaning the house until it sparkled; planting my vegetable gardens with arrow-straight rows and easily weeding out undesirable elements; and vacuuming the carpet into orderly parallel pathways.

Each of these activities required very little thought. My mind could drift and soar. Yet each action created in me a sense of completion. The latter was invaluable as much of my life hung in the balance. The big questions remained entirely unanswered, unknown, and out of my control. As a result, my daily tasks became my elixir.

These simple moments of mindless order and peace felt like exhaling a marvelously contented sigh. I lived so much of my life holding my breath, both literally and figuratively, and to exhale seemed to release the pressure. Quite literally I often had to remind myself to breathe deeply or breathe at all. An intake of breath, the taking in of life, though a basic life function was challenging in my nearly constant fight-flight-freeze modus operandi. When I stopped to center myself with a few slow deep breaths, inner calm and clarity returned.

In those moments I often remembered that I needed care too. Not just Charles. My wounds weren't visible on an x-ray or lab chart. Yet, just like an open sore, they needed attention. Charles had caregivers committed to his care. Near the end of his life I also had unending support, yet my care most often came entirely from me.

Early on I adopted many daily behaviors that provided comfort and allowed me to care for myself. For example, each morning I took a walk no matter the weather. In Charles' final months, that was often the only time I left the house. Hospice volunteers, neighbors and friends came to be with Charles for an hour or two while I marched up and down the nearby county roads, my footsteps a cadence of self care, my mantra and prayer.

And then there were naps. I LOVE to nap, and I partake at every opportunity. My daily naps of 15-30 minutes would calm, refresh and rejuvenate me quickly and gently, like a brief little sortie on a flying carpet.

Quiet moments of writing or prayer in the early morning hours before the house awoke, provided inner calm like the surface of a lake in pre-dawn hours.

Like folding and stacking at my warm clean oasis, these simple moments of much needed self-care provided me a way to *"exhale"* and relax. In hindsight, these activities became tools in my hard knocks tool belt, which I wore so jauntily about my hips. They served me well and allowed me to function, if only for a while.

Chapter Six

—•—

IRON-ON PATCHES

ᔦ

*"How can you follow the course of your life
if you do not let it flow."*
                    - Lao Tsu

ᔦ

ॐ

As a kid I hated iron-on patches. I felt they looked hokey and incredibly tacky. The hole was still evident and the patch simply drew your attention to the hole. What was the purpose? Why ruin a perfectly good pair of jeans just when they started looking really cool? Why must I be tormented so? Why oh why, my little pre-pubescent mind cried out, can't we just leave the hole as it is?

My mother thought in her efficient, practical way that the iron-on patch was the way to go. Interestingly enough, I found myself putting iron-on patches on my heart and soul during our cancer journey. I was numbing, resisting, fearing and turning away from the experience.

To fully experience this journey called cancer requires experiencing a whole rainbow of emotions. There are ups and downs, highs and lows, as well as *"check for a pulse"* in-betweens. This is rarely easy. In fact I found it much easier to simply numb myself in various creative ways. Slap an iron-on patch on the hole in your heart, Elizabeth. While you're at it slap one on the pit in your stomach too. Numbing was rarely a conscious process at first, rather an internal subconscious survival mechanism.

How did I numb me? Let me count the ways. First of all there was action. Task lists and activity were my patches of choice. There was also food, sleep, TV, books, alcohol, gardening, and laundry.

As soon as we received Charles' diagnosis, I sprang into action.

✓ Call friends and relatives.

✓ Call the prayer chain.

✓ Search the internet.

✓ Make doctor appointments.

✓ Keep track of insurance information.

✓ Field countless calls.

✓ Read up on everything imaginable.

✓ Order nutritional supplements.

Oh yes, and while you're at it, do the dishes, clean the house, make all meals, make sure Christopher is O.K., service the car, water the plants, tend to the garden, and continue to keep your home-based business afloat.

It takes an enormous amount of energy to operate in this manner. It is all-consuming and therein lies the key. To go, go, go meant I didn't have to feel, feel, feel.

A very wise woman once told me that resistance is *"pretending what is isn't"*. Think about that for a minute. The *"why me?"* energy, the *"he's so young!"* exclamation, and *"it's just not right"* cry are ways of denying what is. As a friend used to say, *"rocks are hard and water's wet."* The truth was the truth. Charles had cancer. Period. All the patches, the mind-numbing tasks, and contrary exclamations wouldn't change that at all.

Resistance became my middle name. The energy of my resistance those first few years could have powered a dozen major metropolitan areas for an entire decade.

During that time my life-long love affair with food heated up again until it was hot and heavy. Since I was a teen my motto was *pick an emotion, pick a food*. Feeling frustrated, Elizabeth? Have some toast with lots of butter and sugar. Feeling lonely? How about two or three enormous bowls of sugar-sweetened cereal? Feeling sad? How about some Milk Duds or some ice cream or a few dozen cookies?

Sugar was my drug of choice and when Charles became ill I had a legitimate excuse to indulge. Gratefully, I have never been overly heavy. There was a day, however, when I realized I was out of control.

In the fall of 1998, Charles had been receiving

treatment in a Mexican hospital for nearly two weeks with one full week of treatment to go. We were both living at the hospital and the days passed slowly. Time was not measured by the clock, but by each drip of Charles' I.V. Drip, drip, drip, drip.

To ward off boredom, I walked the nearby beach each morning, read much of the day, explored the local shopping area each afternoon and watched TV (sometimes in Spanish) most evenings.

For ten days straight my afternoon walk took me to a nearby drug store. My mission? A box of Milk Duds, comfort in a little yellow box. On the eleventh day, I stood in the candy aisle once again. I realized I didn't bring any money, just a few American pennies left in my pocket from a prior shopping expedition. I distinctly remember contemplating stealing my little yellow friend. Stealing a Box of Milk Duds!

In that moment I despised myself. I realized I had become a person I did not know and a person I certainly did not like. I began to question how an articulate thirty-five year old wife, stepmother and business owner had sunk so low? When did this happen? I was thoroughly disgusted. I left the store and walked the Mexican streets for an hour, a sobbing, soggy gringa, never to return to that store again. Instead, I found other iron-on patches to cover the hurt.

Books were another iron-on patch of choice. While my enormous library of non-fiction absolutely repelled me, I craved a good story. I read romances, mysteries, classics, and foreign tales. I escaped into each page and traveled thousands of miles from the comfort of my armchair.

One day I called the local librarian. I said, *"You know what I like to read. Could you perhaps put together a few books and drop them off at the house?"* (This personalized service is the beauty of living in a small town and knowing everyone quite well.) Charles and I returned the next day from a trip to the doctor to find a large plastic bag of books lying outside the front door under the awning.

I was barely in the door when I gently upended the bag and scattered the books across the floor. I sat down on the floor beside them to touch, feel and read them. I sorted them into *"this one first, now this one, then this one next"* piles. The scene was similar to a child's arrival home after Halloween trick-or-treating. I sat there entranced, immediately transported, and tantalized by the hours of escape and discovery piled before me.

During Charles' final months of care at home, I picked a spot at the dining room table as my throne and place of rest. This is where I spent countless hours reading, or looking out the window, watching the birds, squirrels, and a little red fox that visited frequently. This is where I learned to appreciate the silence. This is where I learned to take off the patches and give my inner wounds the light of day. This is where I learned to simply *"be"*.

My journey taught me that patches are fine but they are meant to be a temporary solution. They are a bridge from one place to another. My patches served to temporarily comfort me but did nothing to heal the broken heart underneath. The patches needed to come off for healing to begin. The wound needed to be exposed and vulnerable to be fully healed.

Chapter Seven

SOAKING

*"Be patient toward all that is unresolved in your heart
and try to love the questions themselves."*
- Rainer Maria Rilke 1875-1926,
Czechoslovakian author

༂

Ever soaked a shirt or trousers with a particularly pesky stain in a cleaning solution, hoping against hope that the claims on the bottle are true? In my life, I have spent hours waiting for the powerful stain fighters to complete their mighty work, sometimes with a desired outcome, sometimes not. Waiting and hoping. Waiting...

Waiting is the part of the cancer journey that perhaps challenged me the most. Being a task driven person, I am not always patient. To wait is to waste time. To wait is to stand impatiently, toe tapping an ancient tribal beat with my sneakered foot, arms folded, lips pursed, brow furrowed and furtive minute-by-minute glances at my free-from-Ragu watch held together by scotch tape with the tomato at 12 o'clock.

Yet, I waited. We waited for everything from hospice volunteers to death. We waited.

I waited on hold for the appointment scheduler at the clinic. We waited for the doctor in a cold and impersonal office as we pretended to focus on a six-month old People magazine. We waited until we were clear about the next treatment method. I waited until

Charles decided on his next course of action. We waited to see how he was feeling before deciding on weekend plans. And, of course, we waited for test results. Wanting the known even if it brought devastating news rather than the abyss of unknown. The latter was nearly excruciating. I remember waiting nearly ninety-six hours (that's four days to the rest of the world) for the results of some particularly important test. Four days... FOUR DAYS!

I had placed so much importance on the outcome of those tests that I surrendered all personal power to the results – commonly known as a medical *opinion*. I allowed the uncertainty of the outcome to determine my mood, my thoughts, and my actions. I put my entire life on hold during those four days – almost like holding my breath. Granted, if you looked at my level of activity during those four days, you'd never know I was mentally out to lunch the entire time. Even though my body was moving at a frenzied pace, and there were countless checks on my task list, my mind was holding its breath, suspended in space waiting for the phone to ring.

Finally the call came from the clinic to deliver the all-important test results. Interestingly enough, it was the delivery of the results, specifically the verbiage, which caught me off guard. A nurse from the doctor's office called to say that Charles' tests "*were negative and the scans were unremarkable".*

Negative and unremarkable.

Allow me to translate: after a course of treatment, there was no detectable cancer and CT scans revealed nothing irregular. A mere 8 months earlier we were advised not to renew magazine subscriptions and now the cancer was gone!

Negative and unremarkable? These are the terms the nurse used for the most positive and incredible results imaginable! In that moment it was clear to me. The objectives of traditional medicine had nothing to do with health but rather the discovery, diagnosis, and management of *disease*. In that same moment, I also asked myself how often I see my life as negative and unremarkable. How often do I disregard or minimize the potent, unimaginable richness & beauty with the mere choice of words? Negative and unremarkable.

We had waited for four days in suspended animation for a negative and unremarkable call. We had waited for the call that would provide a reprieve for a full fourteen months. In that moment it felt as though Charles received a stay of execution and a first class ticket on an express train away from imminent death. Negative and unremarkable.

How often do we take the events of our life and frame them as negative and unremarkable? How often do we surrender our choices to external circumstances or the opinion of others? How often does our language create our experience? How often does our language take us far from an appreciation of the present? Science tells us that the brain takes our words and communicates an experience to the cells in the body setting up a vibration. That vibration is called feeling. How remarkable that our feelings begin with what we tell ourselves about life. Negative and unremarkable.

Fourteen months later the cancer returned and we began another chapter on the cancer journey that led us to the ultimate negative and unremarkable, Charles' death. During the months Charles was in hospice care at home, waiting became the only constant in our lives.

The long afternoons, initially what I called negative and unremarkable, were the worst for me. After lunch was eaten and dishes washed, Charles would not be up for hours and the afternoon hung before me like a silent phantom.

Despite my need for distraction, I refused to get wrapped up in the daytime dramas. After my morning volunteers were gone, the house was quiet as Charles slept. As his wake up time progressed from two o'clock to three to four and then to five, time marched on at a slow motion pace. I worked on the computer, cooked and froze countless soups, and read many, many books.

While the days were long, I gradually came to appreciate the silence and the waiting as it provided access to some of my greatest life lessons. In the silence and in the waiting I learned to be O.K. with my company and myself. I learned to sit still and be patient. I learned to listen. I learned to shift back from a human-doing to a human being. I learned to *"be"* rather that just *"do"*.

This happened not all at once but in spurts and fits. At times I railed against the silence and nearly went mad. Yet, in the end, silence and a patience born of long periods of waiting became my teacher. This happened in part because I surrendered my resistance and moved into the flow of it. I reframed *"negative and unremarkable"* into *"opportunity and rest"* and shifted my reality forever.

In the end, the stakes of waiting seemed so much higher. The texture of the waiting changed and the silence became a potent tangible presence. As we waited for his death, we experienced extraordinary living. Beautiful living in the midst of beautiful dying.

In his final weeks Charles spent his days perched on the windowsill between this life and the next. Most days

Charles hung outside the window ledge by his finger tips with only a shred of Charles remaining in this realm. All I could see were his knuckles during the day but at night he would sit comfortably on the ledge of life and ask for a sandwich. This provided me with some extraordinary emotional calisthenics as I swung from the deepest despair to the greatest joy.

During his final weeks, as Charles would toss and turn, I had trouble rousing him for his meds. His breathing became irregular or non-existent for long stretches. In fact, Charles and I said goodbye to each other in his final months not just once but twelve times. I recall by the tenth time thinking this was startlingly similar to a bad "B" movie.

Each night I slept with one ear open to be sure he was breathing. On a regular basis, all respiration stopped for 15-30 seconds awakening me from my shallow slumber and pulling me to his side. I scooped him in my arms, kissed his brow and whispered words of assurance in his ears that it was alright to go and I would catch up with him later. Not once, not twice, but eleven times, he gasped and gulped a huge breath filling his lungs, then looked up into my face and smiled. Such was our protracted goodbye.

Knowing the death of my husband was approaching while also experiencing remarkable living was an experience unlike any I've ever had. Waiting, previously my own personal worst torture mechanism, became my greatest teacher.

During the quiet, long afternoons I made some sort of small peace with the impending outcome, with our life together, with the many things we shared and those left undone. As all the other voices faded away, I learned to listen to, and deeply appreciate, my own inner voice. I learned that God spoke to me so clearly in those quiet times. All I had to do was sit quietly and listen while diligently guarding what I told myself about my life.

While the medical system strove for life at all costs, as though death is some kind of a failure, I realized it was not. Death is simply a transition, the greatest transition perhaps, and certainly the greatest teacher. Death is a comma, not a period, in a positive and remarkable life. A reward not a punishment. No room for *"negative"* or *"unremarkable"* here.

Then one day, the waiting was over and Charles was gone.

Chapter Eight

SMALL LOADS

"When one door closes another one opens; but we so often look so long and so regretfully upon the closed door, that we do not see the ones which open for us."
- Alexander Graham Bell
1847-1922, Inventor and Teacher of the Deaf

༄

In early January 1999, just six months after Charles' diagnosis, I discovered I was pregnant. Needless to say, this was an enormous shock to us both. We'd been married nearly five years and up until this time, we were both unwilling to open or close that door. In recent months our attention had been elsewhere to be sure.

The mere fact that we never really had open dialogs or made any decisions about having children was actually a telling symptom of our less then stellar communication skills prior to this chapter in our lives. Up to that point we had simply made a decision on this topic by making no decision at all.

On the day I was to get my period, I watched the clock incessantly and made countless bathroom stops. Nevertheless, the day came and went. And the next. and the next... Six days later, I stood in the check out line at the drug store with the pregnancy test in my hands. I made a valiant attempt to look casual while trembling and hoping against hope that I wouldn't see anyone I knew.

My face burned as the clerk, a closet sadist I'm sure,

asked for a price check on EPT At-Home kits over the intercom. I'm sure in that moment, the entire store pretended not to await the reply while stealing quick glances to see what poor fool was being humiliated now.

The disinterested voice of authority regarding all things related to price responded promptly and the store gave a collective embarrassed sigh. Not generally a violent person, I recall long harboring thoughts for the clerk that, if acted upon, would surely allow me the opportunity to experience incarceration.

Hours later, I stood in the bathroom staring in disbelief at the little stick now displaying the most unwelcome pink stripe. Despite reading and re-reading the instructions seeking some kind of caveat, I concluded that I was indeed pregnant. My body, the test, and my intuition hadn't lied. This was really real.

I kept this news to myself for a full twenty-four hours. During that time I pondered all the possibilities in my heart before discussing it with Charles. In hindsight, something told me to simply *be* with this news and fully experience my emotions about it, that this experience was simply about learning and clarifying my life.

Interestingly enough, this twenty-four hour time period

was all I got as I miscarried the following afternoon while Charles was at work. I lay devastated on the bathroom floor sobbing and in pain, overcome with emotion and admittedly relieved.

Charles arrived home from work a few hours later preoccupied and a little bit out of sorts. I put on a brave face and made dinner albeit with little emotion, very much like a robot. I was lost in my own thoughts and feeling decidedly raw. After dinner dishes were cleared and the dishwasher loaded, we assumed our regular assigned spots in the living room. Charles was ensconced in his easy chair, feet up on the ottoman, remote control nearby, with his face covered by the newspaper. I sat on the sofa, feet curled up under a woven blanket, a book in my lap pretending to read.

After an entire sitcom, I took a deep breath and attempted to engage him in a conversation. Achieving only monosyllabic responses and getting rather frustrated, I rose from the sofa. I gently took the newspaper from his hands, shut off the TV and sat on the ottoman immediately in front of him. To his questioning stare I said, *"I need your attention, honey. We have something really important we need to discuss."*

I told him the story of the preceding twenty-four hours and watched a parade of emotions march across his face. The pain on his face was undeniable, mixed with concern for me and his own grief intertwined with undeniable relief.

After giving him a few moments of silence to let it all sink in, I said, *"Honey, this is a long overdue conversation and I need you to answer a question for me as honestly as you can."* In that moment, I can only imagine what he was feeling.

Another deep breath and I continued. *"On a scale of one to one hundred, where one is no and one hundred is yes, where are you on the whole having kids thing?"*

Silence...

"Precious," I said, *"please know that there are no wrong or right answers here. I simply need to know where you are on this? We can no longer afford to simply not talk about these really important things."*

"One is no and one hundred is yes, right?" he asked. His eyes were tear-stained and his voice was thick with emotion.

"Un huh." I said, never taking my eyes off his troubled face.

I believe this was the question he feared answering

since the day we met. Our nearly six year age difference and his previous marriage that had produced a wonderful, nearly grown son were now fully present and no longer easily ignored. Front and center stood the truth simply awaiting voice and breath.

He was silent for nearly one full minute. I too remained silent patiently awaiting his response. When he finally spoke his voice was somewhat choked and tight, barely audible at a whisper.

"Twenty," he whispered, the word a nearly inaudible exhale. That number, that word, and all it represented, hung heavily in the air between us like a dense spring fog.

He continued, now somewhat relieved of this burden by speaking his thoughts aloud. *"I would love any child of ours. You know that, don't you? But I have a child. My son is nearly grown and he's absolutely marvelous. I've done the whole 'diaper routine' so long ago. Most importantly, while I want to believe I'll be fine and my health will remain strong, we simply don't know the outcome of this chapter of our lives. That's as honest as I can be."*

He flashed me the most loving, albeit pained, smile and then asked me, *"And you, sweetie, where are you in all this?"*

It was my turn to speak that which I had avoided speaking for our entire marriage and what my thirty-five year old body had been telling me for quite some time.

"Fifty", I said. Right in the middle.

We sat holding hands and avoiding each other's eyes for what seemed like forever, in reality only three minutes. The clock on the wall ticked a barely audible beat gently accompanying the cat's soft purring. The January wind lashed at the hanging ornament just outside the front door creating a percussive rhythmic clank.

"Those aren't very good odds, are they honey?" I finally asked. *"Any child of ours deserves more than that. Yet this is where we are. This is how we feel. Neither of us is right or wrong here. We simply are in different places. It is pretty darn clear now. How about we gently set that dream aside for now and focus on you being healthy?"*

He looked at my tear-streaked face and quietly folded me into his arms. We both sat and cried for quite a long time, gently rocking each other for comfort until the tears stopped and our need for tissue drove us apart.

Later that night, I cried myself to sleep before Charles

came to bed, hating the cancer that created such uncertainty in our lives, yet almost grateful for an excuse not to travel the path of motherhood. I felt empty, yet clear. I felt unmistakable grief laced with profound inner peace.

Just before drifting off I remember being grateful to the cancer for teaching us to communicate and for teaching us honesty, for teaching us the power of open dialog and the ability to honor each other's views. Our once-hated presence had become our most valuable teacher.

Chapter Nine

MAXIMUM AGITATION

*"The fastest way to freedom
is to feel your feelings."*
- Gita Bellin
Author, **Amazing Grace**

၇

How do you get mad at someone who is dying? I guess the proverbial tongue-in-cheek answer "*very carefully*" works here as well as any. One part of this journey that I found tremendously incongruent and challenging to express was my feelings of anger toward Charles during his illness.

It wasn't that it was tough to be angry, there are plenty of things in *any* marriage that can make a gal a little grouchy now and again. (Girls, think toilet seats and remote controls.) What challenged me most was feeling that I had the right to be angry with him at all. After all, the guy's got cancer, right? He should be handled with loving kid gloves. I should be a saint and just let it all roll off my back, right? WRONG!

Calling all caregivers! Hear me well. Despite all the *"shoulds"* your friends, family, and neighbors may hand you, please remember you get to have ALL of your feelings. You get to feel, in fact I encourage you, the complete myriad of emotions that present themselves during this journey. There will be anger, love, sadness, passion, desperation, tenderness, and even rage. I now understand these emotions are remarkably normal. In fact, I imagine they are normal in a marriage that doesn't include cancer. They should be doubly normal in this intensely challenging emotional time as well. While I know this now, I didn't know it when I was knee deep in the experience. As a result, I didn't allow myself to admit I felt much of anything, let alone anger, during those first few years. I put on my fiercely determined, loving face and wore it like a treasured mask.

Anger has long been a challenging area for me. We didn't express it much in my home as I was growing up. We had articulate "*discussions*" instead and we rarely raised our voices. This went on until the passive aggressive behavior fueled a steady boil and all hell broke loose for a good old shout-fest. Short, intense, and rather noxious, always from my mouth, hurled at my parents.

As difficult as it is for me to admit, I found myself angry with Charles at different times during his long illness. Right out of the chute, when we first found out he had cancer, I was livid. Logical or not, I was just plain self-righteously pissed off.

Esophageal cancer is almost completely preventable. As is most cancer, it is linked directly to diet and lifestyle in most cases. Obesity, a sedentary lifestyle, eating late at night and lying on the sofa, eating lots of sweets are contributing factors to chronic heartburn and indigestion which can lead to esophageal cancer.

Charles was the king of all these habits and behaviors. He was overweight, loved sweets, and would take them intravenously if he could. He loved to fall asleep on the sofa each night, TV remote in hand and a cherry lifesaver tucked in his cheek, after a large bowl of ice cream.

I remember one night shortly before he was diagnosed, we had an argument. I had been encouraging him for a few years to exercise and take better care of his body. It fell on deaf ears.

On this particular evening Charles sat in his easy chair, his nightly ice cream *"fix"* propped on his belly, the TV on full-blast playing one mindless sitcom while taping another to be viewed later, and the newspaper covering his face. After hearing him complain yet again about heartburn, I distinctly recall standing up directly in front of his chair, yanking away the paper, looking directly in his eyes, saying, *"What's it going to take, Charles? Do you have to get cancer before you make some changes in your life?"*

Yes, I really said that. Ouch and double ouch. Are you cringing too?

I stayed angry with him for months after he was

diagnosed. Not so you'd know it on the outside but on the inside I was furious. To be honest, however, I was simply terrified and anger was how it showed up in my life. While the type-A controlling part of me raced to manage all the details and find a cure or a solution, another part of me felt scared and helpless. At some level I chose to experience and express the latter as self-righteous anger.

One day, about four months after diagnosis, I awoke with a question in my heart. *"If he dies tomorrow, is this how I want our final time together to feel?"* Boy, did that ever put things into perspective. Denying my feelings while also harboring and not expressing them in a healthy way, was polluting our relationship and my entire life. In fact, at a time when I craved closeness in our marriage, I was driving him away.

With that realization, I began the process of releasing Charles to his experience and owning my judgment, fears and feelings as mine. He wasn't the cause of these feelings. I was. In fact, they weren't about him but rather about me. The saying, *"It is never what happens, it is what I choose to do with it"*, rang in my ears from that day forward.

Interestingly enough, by the summer of 2001, a few short months before his death, I had yet another chance to learn this lesson.

By July 2001, Charles was able to work only four or five hours per day (down from his normal ten to twelve) and he was consistently in pain. He began experiencing severe headaches as well as severe back and chest pain; eating became more difficult and he slept more and more each day. His body, originally a hearty two hundred pounds, was now struggling to tip the scales at one hundred forty-five.

With the amount of care he required, the sheer number of details that required attention around the house, financial matters and attending to family, I was exhausted mentally and physically. He needed hospice care. Just as importantly, so did I.

Despite the fact that he was often so weak he couldn't walk the three hundred yards from his office to the house, he fought the idea of hospice care like an enraged bull. He was angry with me for suggesting he needed it and he shut me out as his way of protest. He was angry. So was I. In reality we were both hurt and scared.

For Charles, hospice signified the end and surrender to the cancer which he had fought so hard for so very long. He thought hospice meant he was weak, that he had lost. For me it meant support, better care than I could provide and no more pretending that everything was O.K. With two such diverse perspectives, was it any wonder we argued? Interestingly enough, this was our last argument.

It was Charles who finally created a truce. In his selfless manner, he was the one to look outside himself for the answer. One evening he looked at me, really looked closely, and for the first time in a long time, saw the exhausted eyes, the weary body, the worried brow. Even as his own body was failing, his love for me recognized the need for surrender. And he did.

When he surrendered, he surrendered completely. He surrendered to care. He surrendered to waiting. He surrendered to his life. He surrendered to his death. He let go of his ego but never his dignity. In his final months he invited people into his life and cared for their souls as they cared for his body. As a result, he opened to the world the beauty of his death and taught all whom he touched a grace I have not seen since.

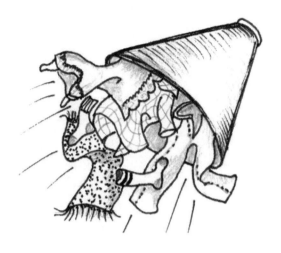

Chapter Ten

SHOUT IT OUT

"The strongest oak tree of the forest is not the one that is protected from the storm and hidden from the sun. It's the one that stands in the open where it is compelled to struggle for its existence against the winds and rains and the scorching sun."
- Napoleon Hill
1883-1970, Author, **Think and Grow Rich**

ॐ

A friend of mine died almost exactly 5 months before Charles. He'd been sick for quite some time and most recently in the hospital. He seemed to be rallying, just like so many times before. But it all snuck up on him. It was simply too much. Scotty was thirty-nine years old. His partner, Rob, had been my best friend for over nineteen years. The four of us were close, linked in many ways but most keenly by a common experience of living with serious illness. Scotty's death hit so very close to home.

Charles brought me the news as I was standing in my garden, dirty, dusty, blissful, and sweaty. As the words began to sink into my blue-sky afternoon, I began to ask myself over and over, *"What do I do with this news? Can this possibly be true?"* Scotty's death just didn't figure into my thinking. You see, if Scotty could die then Charles could too, an option I was unwilling to accept despite the probability.

It made no sense. How was I supposed to deal with the emotions that wanted to gobble me up and spit me out? How was I supposed to respond to a situation that no words could change and, in all probability, awaited me at some unknown future date? In the midst of it all, I was aching for Rob. I wanted to be with him, comfort him, listen to and help him. I wanted to be a friend to him and be there for support. Yet, I am not proud to say that Scotty's death became more about Charles and me than about Rob and Scott.

As I stood there in the garden, with Charles watching closely, I wondered where to turn when I didn't even know who or what I needed? Normally I would turn to Charles as I had done for our entire marriage. Yet, in this situation, I was hesitant to show him my utter and complete devastation. I wanted to show him that I could be strong. That's what I wanted him to see, but not what I showed him.

My response? I got in the car, rolled up all the windows, and drove nearby country roads, screaming, wailing and hollering. I was shocked by the sounds that emanated from within me, *Wild Kingdom* fans would have been impressed. For miles I continued to shout and wail.

I recall feeling grateful for the motion of the car, so I drove and drove. I surrendered to my grief and embraced the freedom of release. I hollered until my eyes ached, my head hurt, and my throat was sore. I was spent. Empty. Raw. Twenty-five miles later I was finally at peace.

This was the first time I got a taste of unbounded grief. I wasn't crying just for Scott and for Rob, I was crying for me and for Charles. I experienced a taste of what was to come. Scotty's death opened within me a well of emotion that I had held at bay thus far. It cracked the seal and my insides poured out with astonishing force threatening to carry me away.

In my spent state, I also glimpsed the ebb and flow of even the most intense storms of emotion. This was somehow soothing. It was reassuring to know that I could go into my darkest places and trust I would come out, perhaps battered but intact.

Rob was the one who shared with me the most profound piece of wisdom I have ever heard. Shortly after he learned of Charles' diagnosis he said, *"Charles will do this journey differently than you would. Let him have his experience. Don't forget that his way is right too. Maybe not for you, but it is exactly right for him and he gets to choose it."* After four years of Scott's illness, these words came from a deep well of personal understanding.

It took me three years to thoroughly understand that wisdom and release Charles to his experience. Early on, though, I recognized the truth in his words. And frankly, I hated it.

It would have been so easy for me, the Type-A controller, to *"manage his case"* and remain comfortably behind the *"task list"* clipboard. When I really understood what Rob said to me, I knew that this clinical and detached way of operating would not serve either one of us.

While I knew Charles and I shared this journey to a point, the trajectory of Charles' path was not mine, but entirely his. Charles got to decide who he was in the face of cancer and how he would live and quite possibly die. He alone could decide how he would allow the experience to change, transform and mold him. That was not for me to control or manage.

In rereading what I've written, I fear I've made letting go sound easy. This is not my intention because for me it was not. *"Aaaargh!"* was the oft-heard battle cry of my highly frustrated, type-A, planning, strategizing and organizing warrior. I was not in control of Charles. I was responsible only for me and for my response! The only thing worse would have been if you took away my multi-tabbed day planner and made me watch as you burned it.

In the end, I managed the medicine schedule, the bathing schedule, the volunteer schedule and thousands of details with a tenacity and precision that amazes me even today. I let go, however, of managing

Charles and his experience. This happened a little at a time until at last I let go in his final days.

The letting go process, the release of control of another human being, brought with it profound waves of grief paired with a silent peace. I am grateful for this lesson and carry it with me today as a valuable tool and wise instructor.

Chapter Eleven

QUARTERS

"Turn your troubles into treasures.
Learn from them and grow from them."
                    - Mark Victor Hansen
            Author, **Chicken Soup For The Soul**

ഗ

Cancer is expensive. Prevention is cheap. Waiting until you have it is costly. How's that for irony in its finest moment? Yet in our country, the brunt of the attention is given to disease, focused not on prevention but treatment. Charles and I discovered that we now have a medical system that is so closely linked to costly technology and enormous amounts of bureaucracy, that the traditional path of treatment is staggeringly expensive.

When Charles was diagnosed we were living on a shoestring budget. I was starting a business, and Charles' salary was not very large. We were stretched pretty thin most of the time. We quickly realized that we would have to invite people into our story and ask them for help. I had been operating most of my life as a type-A controller while Charles was a very private analytical type. We realized that now was not the time for our pride to derail us. We needed help.

A friend at our church suggested we write an article for the weekly newsletter to the congregation, and we did. In it we outlined Charles' health challenges to be sure, but we also spoke of our belief in the possibility of recovery. While somewhat controversial, we made no apology for our choices of unconventional treatment mixed with traditional methods and simply asked for their prayers and help.

It wasn't enough to do the impossible and ask for help. When help arrived we had to learn to receive. As a result of that article, we received abundant support, financially and otherwise, from countless sources. Support showed up from family, friends, people we knew well and those we didn't know at all. As support flowed in, I became keenly aware of how living a decent life, how caring about others, how ministering to them and loving them, was coming back to Charles many times over.

Cancer was an opportunity for both of us to take a close look at our deeply held beliefs about money. We both realized that we were carrying around shame about our financial status. We recognized that our beliefs about money were not serving us in our desire to create greater financial abundance to see us through this storm.

Charles filed bankruptcy a few months before we were married. He felt so very guilty about it. He wore it like an invisible badge of disgrace that only he could see yet it obstructed his view of life. As he sat in his chair, working on our bills, he would sigh long and loud with a note of resignation. He gave much of his energy to clipping coupons, filling out rebates and finding discounts on everything from toothpaste to razors.

Charles' beliefs about money also influenced his choices pertaining to his own medical care. The prospect of paying even the patient *"co-pay"* amount made it almost physically painful for him to have a medical test, despite being potentially critical to his survival. In fact, he admitted many times that he didn't go to the doctor sooner when he suspected something was wrong for this very reason.

I, too, had some beliefs about money that became evident during Charles' illness. For as long as I can remember, I believed that those with wealth were somehow different. Growing up, our dinner conversations about families or individuals with money were conducted with reverence. People who were doctors, lawyers, or graduates of respected universities were held in high esteem and spoken of in hushed tones. I am not proud to say that I adopted an attitude somewhere along the way that people without money were to be looked on with pity or even a *"shouldn't they know better?"* air. I was offered a new perspective when we temporarily became *them* for a while.

In the face of the beliefs we brought to our marriage, it is amazing that we **always** had enough, one way or another. Truly a sign of the abundance of life.

Sadly, Charles' fear of not having enough was nearly crippling at times. In fact, I saw this belief create in him a near paralysis and a very real isolation. He didn't join the local bowling group because he didn't want to spend the five dollars per week. He didn't have many close friends because he didn't want to waste gas or money going out to activities or events. He allowed money, or his perceived lack of money and the shame he attached to that perception, to create a nearly impenetrable wall around him. The result was that he knew countless people and was loved and respected, but Charles had very few close friends he let inside.

Our journey with cancer brought us face to face with these beliefs. We were invited to hold up each belief and look at it closely, often in the harshest light. We were invited to assess its value to the direction of our dreams, to retain or discard it with a discerning eye, not simply with the programming from our childhood.

Along the way we began to see money as a faithful servant and not the limited commodity or unforgiving master we believed. We finally saw money as a tool to provide comfort, a mechanism for giving, a method of exchange, and a key to the door of opportunity. In this realization, the doors of abundance were thrown open, allowing it to flow.

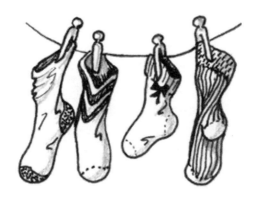

Chapter Twelve

THE SOCK ABYSS

*"If you are never scared, embarrassed or hurt,
it means you never take chances."*
- Julia Soul, Actress

❧

So what's the deal with socks and laundry? I know you know what I mean. Where does that one sock go? I *know* I put both socks in the laundry basket. I'm *sure* they both went into the washer. The washer and dryer are only *three* inches apart. How can it be that only one sock emerges from the clutches of the dryer, not just once but time and time again? Where do they all go, those many little socks?

There must be itty-bitty sock gremlins living within my dryer. Perhaps the little sock eaters ride around in microscopic space ships on the warm drying currents seeking opportunities for mischief and masterminding ways to create chaos. While not terribly likely, the explanation works for me as I fold my whites.

I remember the day I realized the sock gremlins had started smuggling out some of my thoughts as well as various cotton attire. They ransacked Charles' brain too, more so at the end. We became so forgetful at one point, all we could do was laugh. Yet under the laughter was a river of sadness and an awareness that the progression of the disease impacted us both.

Charles was one of the sharpest people I ever knew.

His intellectual capacity was astonishing. His grasp of strategy, facts, and figures astounded everyone he knew. His razor sharp memory was something he was quite proud of and exercised it constantly recalling facts and dates and names. Despite all this, there came a time when I realized that the cancer was affecting not just his body but also his prized mental faculties. This awareness came packed in a simple exchange.

I asked Charles if he would like to eat some toast. To this question, he responded *"Why yes, that would be nice dear. With honey on it, please."* When I brought it to him just a few minutes later, he said a little testily, *"I didn't ask for this. Take it away. I'm not hungry."*

This may seem like a small thing and in a way it was. This incident was, however, the first clear example that something wasn't quite right with Charles' mental processing. As I stood by Charles' chair holding a plate of toasted bread, images flashed through my mind of previously dismissed oddities. I recalled such things as finding items in really odd places. For example two days prior I found the TV remote control in the refrigerator. I suddenly saw the growing clutter of Charles' home office space through different eyes. It all added up differently and was the first time I felt my husband slipping away. What I later referred to as *"the toast incident"* was a blow to my optimism and hope for his recovery.

In the final weeks of Charles' life, my mental process took a startling hit as well. The sheer number of Charles' prescriptions soared weekly as new and troubling symptoms surfaced and took hold. Countless bottles were lined up like toy soldiers on the kitchen counter, each with cryptic instructions understood clearly by only a select few. Some medications were to be taken daily while others every third day. Some were taken around the clock while others were to be administered only in the morning. Liquids and tablet, pills and caplets had their own purpose and order requiring attention to detail and military precision that we managed with lists and hand-drawn posted schedules.

Late one Friday night Charles awoke in a sweat-drenched delirium. He complained of a headache and inability to sleep. Earlier that week the hospice nurse told me this was a possible side effect of all that was happening inside his skin. She delivered a pill the doctor thought would possibly provide relief.

In the middle of the night, I searched the house for instruction for this balm. I was *certain* she said to give him a whole pill then wait thirty minutes to assess the results. If no improvement occurred, another half pill was to follow. I followed these instructions to the letter. A few days later I remembered what she actually said. In reality she told me to start with *one-half* pill, wait *ninety* minutes and if the desired results did not occur, then try something else.

I spent the remainder of that night unsuccessfully trying to calm Charles' increasing agitation. An hour later I must have briefly dozed off and awoke to find him wandering around the house, muttering incoherently. For five more hours he talked animatedly and incessantly in a language only he could understand. He tried to get up and walk around every three to five minutes, tottering precariously on his weakened legs and feet that had been assisted in recent weeks by a shiny silver wheelchair.

This went on in various forms for thirty-six hours. When Sunday afternoon arrived the Charles I knew began to emerge from his medicated fog. He was certain it was Saturday and was horrified to find that he lost nearly an entire weekend. He remembered nothing except going to bed on Friday night.

This pharmaceutical debacle happened only once, yet pains me to this day. I worked for so long and labored so hard to provide comfort, alleviate problems and reduce Charles' pain. Yet it was my own hands that caused this crisis to occur. I had been so focused on Charles' increasing frailty, yet this episode pointed out to me a frailty of my own. Somewhere along the line a mental connection was lost inside me, common sense took a vacation, and clear thinking temporarily vanished.

Where did it go? The sock abyss perhaps?

Chapter Thirteen

SEPARATES

"The best and most beautiful things in the world cannot be seen or touched... but are felt in the heart."
                                                    - Helen Keller 1880-1968

ॐ

On October 9, after two months in Hospice care, Charles and I spent the last night together in our bed. His medication and the slow starvation process had caused such severe jerking and twitching that I was getting no sleep. He agreed to get a hospital bed.

I remember the first night the bed was there in our room, parallel to our bed, separated by four feet. Those four feet might well have been four miles. As I prepared him for bed, then got myself ready for bed, a strange feeling was present in the room. It was later than usual as we had both been avoiding going to sleep in our new separate locations.

Once he was situated in the bed where he would eventually take his last breath, a great sadness washed over me. I crawled into our (now my) bed and we faced one another. His skinny arm slowly reached across for mine.

"I don't like this, sweetie", he whispered.

"Me neither," was my response.

Then we quietly lay there, our fingers barely able to

touch, more connected than ever and separated by the crevasse now between us.

For me, our bed was always a safe place of comfort, warmth, peace, affection, rest and joy. On countless nights, I curled up behind Charles and formed myself to his big strong back. In the early morning hours he would do the same, wrapping his arms around me and holding me close. Now our bed was too large, too cold, and far too empty.

I had pushed for the hospital bed, just as I pushed for most everything. Intellectually I knew it was the right thing to do, providing Charles greater possibilities and ease of function in his ever-increasing number of sleeping hours. Yet I never acknowledged these four feet would break my heart.

In hindsight, I wonder how it felt for Charles that night? Did he feel I was pushing him away? Did he feel as alone as I did as we lay in our separate beds four feet apart?

On our annual July family trip to the north shore of Lake Superior, it felt as though Charles was *"separate"* there as well. He slept nearly the entire trip. Our lovely Lake Superior cottage bedroom was his home for much of the four-day retreat. Christopher and I hiked with my family, made trips into Grand Marais, watched movies as it rained and played cards for hours. Charles slept much of the time in our bedroom. At least he was here, I reasoned.

I can only imagine the sense of isolation he felt back in the bedroom, there at the cabin and at home as well. Separated, out of sight, and tucked away. While I was sure it was for him, for his privacy and comfort, I now wonder if it was for me as well? Did I simply not want to witness his slow and painful death every hour of the day?

For me the greatest challenge of this intensely emotional time was separating out the feelings. There are so many emotions that coexisted, at times it was hard for me to recognize myself or my feelings.

The question at the forefront of my mind, from the depth of my love for him, was ALWAYS, "W*hat's best for Charles?"* Yet, I see now that the question I quietly asked of myself was, *"What's best for me?"* Sadly, many times those questions became confused and intertwined making decisions exceedingly murky and enormously challenging.

A few years ago, my mom and dad celebrated their fiftieth anniversary. My parents, two brothers, Charles, Christopher and I went to a lovely lakeside Minnesota resort for a long weekend celebration. One evening I asked mom and dad about the secret of a long successful marriage.

"Oh, I know", said my father. *"I know the secret!"*

"Yes, dad?" I asked. *"What is the secret?"*

"The secret of our long and successful marriage is that each night I warm up your mother's side of the bed!" he replied with a twinkle in his eyes.

Each night my father gets ready for bed before my mother and climbs into her side of the bed. When she comes to bed, he moves to his side and she crawls into a nicely warmed bed. Isn't that magnificent?

I realized in that moment that it wasn't about warming up the bed. It was about serving the ones you love from a place of love. It was about choosing to serve from the heart, not from obligation or *"should"*.

What an extraordinary lesson! I carried that lesson with me on my journey with Charles and it served me well. In fact, I believe it served us both well. Despite the moments of disconnection, pain and separateness inherent in this journey, our love, respect, and complete devotion to each other wove a triple braided chord that links us forever.

Chapter Fourteen

———•———

RINSE AND REMINISCE

*"Autumn is a second spring when
every leaf is a flower."*
- Albert Camus, 1913-1960
Playwright and novelist

෧

In mid-October, roughly five weeks before Charles passed away, we took the most marvelous extended vacation. We traveled thousands of miles, saw countless beautiful vistas, and explored other countries. All from the comfort of his hospital bed.

Autumn in Minnesota was unseasonably warm with long, sunny days and crisp cool evenings. The gold, red, green, and orange foliage outside our window created a golden light and timelessness in our bedroom each afternoon. This softened the jarring presence of the oxygen machine, bed pan, wheel chair and other accouterment associated with in-home hospice care.

Charles was primarily confined to his bed at this time due to his weakness and fatigue. He passed his days with a white sheet pulled up over his waist or tucked up under his arms, and his head slightly inclined, asleep or dozing in and out, perched between this life and the next.

One particularly lovely afternoon I slipped into his room and watched him sleep. Shortly he awoke and sensed my presence, his eyes lighting up as he saw me. He reached out his hand to me. I took it and gently crawled into bed with him snuggling into his warmth, treasuring the closeness. We held each other for a very long time, listening to the sounds of each other's breathing, saying volumes without the need of words.

As I looked around the room, the golden light playing on the walls, I noticed a souvenir we had picked up on a cruise we enjoyed the preceding winter. I pointed it out to Charles and we began to remember aloud that wonderful adventure. I conjured each detail of the trip and softly recounted them as we held one another. He smiled and nodded, adding little but enjoying the narrative. Thus began a lovely adventure seen only on the screen of our minds yet experienced with loving emotion, remembered joy, and deepest gratitude.

After our cruise, we went to a small island in Florida where we spent ten lovely days walking the beach, listening to the waves, napping each afternoon, and reveling in each other's company. From our golden roost on the mechanized bed, we heard the waves again, felt the sand beneath our feet, tasted the salt air and felt the lap of the waves on our legs as we stood in the water each evening to watch the sunset.

From Florida we traveled to Colorado where we hiked the San Juan National Forest outside Pagosa Springs. We climbed the rocks to Cliff Palace in Mesa Verde. We crossed the suspension bridge at Royal Gorge and then flew to San Diego where we felt the sun on Coronado Island. We heard the lazy river lap the sides of our canoe in northern Arkansas, and watched in awe the grand waves of Lake Superior. My head was full of beautiful images as my heart overflowed with gratitude for each experience, now a priceless treasure in my heart. Charles seemed peaceful and content to hold me as we traveled from this haven of warmth.

On September 11, 2001, Charles knew he was dying. When he heard the news of the terrorist attacks on the World Trade Center, he was devastated. In the following days, he saw the many grief stricken faces of those holding photos as well as hope for their loved one's safe return. He called me to him as the rawest of emotions played out across the TV screen. He took my hand and, with tears in his eyes, said, *"We are so blessed, honey."*

"We are what'" I thought? We are so blessed?! I was taken aback for a moment, but only a moment. We **were** so blessed. We were given the most rare precious gift. We were given the opportunity to say to each other everything in our hearts, to travel together the roads that had brought us great joy, and to say goodbye. We were complete. Indeed we were blessed.

Chapter Fifteen

THE LINT TRAP

"The road is wide and the stars are out
and the breath of the night is sweet,
And this is the time when wanderlust
should seize upon my feet.
But I'm glad to turn from the open road
and the starlight on my face,
And leave the splendor of the out-of-doors
for a human dwelling place."
    - Joyce Kilmer, 1886-1918
    American Poet

ക

P erhaps one of the greatest inventions in the highly complex world of laundry is the lint trap on the dryer. As everything tumbles round and round, this splendid invention picks up the debris that would otherwise clog the entire system and gently separates it out to be tossed away later. Such a simple thing really, yet so remarkably necessary for long-term effectiveness and efficient operation.

As I tumbled through this experience I became aware that my friends and family played the critical role of *lint trap* in my life. They completely surrounded me with warmth and gently absorbed all that would clog my thinking, such as frustration and aggravation, disappointment and pain. They received it and carried it away from me, disposing of it properly with the power of their love.

For months on end, every day brought something special to warm my life and brush away some of the sorrow, such as an e-mail or phone call, a brief note or care package, a hug and a pot of tea, or listening ear. Those around us provided quiet service as they cooked and cleaned the house, sat with Charles so I could take a walk, and prayed unceasingly for our entire family.

They shared the fleeting moments of joy and absorbed my frustrated ranting and tearful despair. Their gifts were freely given and their generosity was unending.

Those closest to me helped sort through the many emotions that co-existed so tumultuously in my heart. As I wrestled with the ever-present questions, *"Am I doing this right?"* and *"Am I doing enough?"* they gently reassured me that my actions were indeed right and enough. They reminded me that it had to be right, it had to be enough, because it was my very best. To ponder otherwise through the eyes of self-recrimination and perfectionism served nothing and no one, becoming a subtle form of self-abuse.

Yet, day after day I beat myself senseless with my own expectations. So often I became mired in the belief that Charles' life was somehow up to me and I could save him. Countless nights I lay awake searching for the key that would liberate him from pain and keep him alive. My friends brought me back to reality as they reminded me that I was human and God was in charge, despite my self-important musings to the contrary.

The expectations I had for myself were enormous. My attempts to be all things to all people required me to be upbeat, strong and focused when I wanted to cry and sleep. A harsh unforgiving inner voice demanded that the house needed to be clean at all times and if it wasn't it reflected poorly on my character. I believed the refrigerator had to be constantly full and ready for unexpected guests. I put upon myself the task of ensuring all family members were included, cared for and emotionally stable. Caregiving took many forms and filled every waking moment.

I see now that I derived a sense of deep satisfaction playing the role of super-woman. Despite not being able to save my husband, to the outside world I appeared to have it all together. I quietly swelled with pride when those who didn't know me well said, *"You're doing so well! How do you do it?"*

In the midst of my madness, there were those who saw the truth underneath the façade I showed to the outside world. They regularly took me aside and gently, without judgment, held up the mirror for me to see myself. They uncovered the frightened girl cowering just below the surface. They provided a safe place for her to rest and they loved her unconditionally.

One week before Charles died, I accepted an invitation to spend three days at a friend's house twenty-five miles from home. A small group was gathering from all around the country for a retreat at my friend's farm. Charles' sister, Anne, a nurse, was with him and I knew she would call if his condition changed. Even so, the waves of guilt I felt for leaving him often threatened to engulf me. Anne and my friends assured me he was in good hands and suggested that the best way to care for Charles at that moment was to care for myself.

During those three days, my friends and I had a marvelous retreat. The days were filled with rest, good food, intelligent conversation, and ease. Charles was stable and well cared for in my short absence and I returned to his side, refreshed and ready for his final days.

Charles had a lint trap too, his colleague and best friend, Sue. Her friendship was to both of us a blessing and a cure. At times, I recognized he needed something I could not give and Sue was there. Her daily presence and cheerful disposition filled our home with light and chased out worry for a while.

In Sue Charles found a place where he was able to safely speak his deepest darkest fears, something he rarely chose to do with me in an effort to protect me. At times I found it challenging to accept that I could not be Charles' *"everything"*, yet looking at my own life I saw that I needed others as well.

Most challenging for me were those moments when I understood that Charles needed something no human being could give. His path would be determined by God and by him, not by the doctors or by me. In these rare moments I understood that ultimate healing would come to Charles only in his death and I began to let go. Those closest to me helped bear the resulting grief and shoulder the sadness.

My friends and family saved me from complete self-destruction. Their gifts were generous and copious, yet distilled down to one: they loved me not because of what I did or didn't do. They very simply loved me just as they found me, exactly as I was.

Their persistent care and attention to my inner functioning helped to clear away all that would hinder my recovery. Their presence laid a foundation for the healing I am experiencing today.

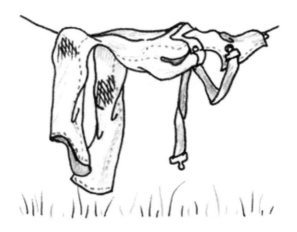

Chapter Sixteen

GRASS STAINS

"Atlas was not forced to hold up the world. He was
convinced that if he didn't, the world would fall."
- Mark Nepo, author,
The Book of Awakening

O n November 10, 2001, just 12 days before Charles' death, I took the ride of my life. For one hour I was a Harley Momma, purple leather and all.

Some friends of mine are Harley folk, complete with leather outfits, gloves, helmets, boots, glasses, and all the associated accessories required of such weekend warriors. During the week they do all the things others do, such as go to the dentist, buy groceries, pay taxes, care for the yard and cook meals. On the weekend, however, my friends take to the road on their mighty stallions made of steel as the engines roar, the wind blows and the miles tick away.

During Charles' final weeks, my friend, Leslie, and I would talk every few days. We would often discuss the challenges I experienced due to my current loss of freedom brought on by the constant nature of home hospice care. I frequently shared the challenges I was experiencing with my friend who cared for both her sister and mother in their final weeks.

She listened as I ranted about how challenging I found the silence of the house, the slowness of each day, the hurry up and wait of the dying process, and the fatigue associated with experiencing a cornucopia of emotions all at once. For one who lived a life of perpetual *doing*, just *being* still and waiting was an enormous challenge for me. Thank goodness for Leslie, who understood it all.

One day she said, *"How would you like a ride on the bike some sunny day? Riding gave me a sense of freedom during my challenging times and I'd love to share that experience with you. I could stay with Charles while my friend takes you for a ride. Just an hour or so. How would you like that?"*

My policy on motorcycles has long been that I would ride one just as long as I had a written guarantee from God that I wouldn't get hurt. Actually, just a phone call or e-mail from God would probably do the trick. This time, however, the allure of a brief adventure and a small breath of freedom, along with my friend's sincere desire to do something nice for me, compelled me to say *"yes"*. When everything within me said, *"no"* I said *"yes"*.

They showed up in the middle of a sunny Saturday afternoon. The weather was perfect, an odd November in Minnesota complete with sunny warm days and absolutely no snow. Upon arrival, Leslie leapt out of her purple leather outfit and promptly helped me leather up. Shortly I was donning a helmet, glasses, scarf, vest, jacket, chaps, boots, and gloves. I was a vision in purple from head to toe, looking mighty fine, if I must say so myself.

I left Charles in Leslie's very capable and experienced hands, tucked my cell phone in my pocket and headed off down the road astride a Harley. I was filled with excitement and an overwhelming sense of foreboding.

For forty glorious minutes we were free. We sailed down quiet country lanes, the bike easily swaying with the curve of the road. Due to the unseasonable warmth, the muted colors of fall still lingered in places creating a magnificent autumn tableau for our viewing pleasure as we crisscrossed the county. I recall feeling a mixture of absolute freedom and exhilaration paired with unquestionable terror. Not being at the wheel, I felt completely out of control yet I didn't really care, hurtling down the road in my purple attire with the sun on my face.

About forty minutes after it began, the ride came to an abrupt end as we skidded into a ditch at 45 miles per hour and rolled end over end until we came to an abrupt stop cradled among the fall-brown grasses.

The bike was severely damaged, its parts littering the ditch and lying tangled among the weeds. We were both bruised from head to toe, in fact, I believe even my hair sustained some damage. Glasses and cell phones were lost or destroyed, yet we both walked out of the ditch on our own volition. An absolute miracle if you ask me. No doubt someone was watching over us. Perhaps someone who clung to life a few miles away?

Some local folks came to our rescue a few minutes later and graciously provided us a ride back home. As we hobbled into the house and as she realized what happened, a sheer look of horror completely overtook my friend's face. She was mortified. Her gesture of kindness had somehow gone wrong.

Funny, I knew intuitively not to go on that ride even before we left the driveway. My heart screamed *"no"* as my head said *"yes"*. I listened to my intuition in so many instances in my life, yet I didn't listen here. I listened when it spoke of how to care for Charles or how to be a friend to Christopher. I listened when it told me how to best involve the family, about when to hang on and even when to let go. Yet, from this place of desperation and mind-numbing fatigue, I did not listen. I was simply too tired.

Now I see that I wanted out and not just out of the house. I wanted out of it all. I wanted out of the pain, out of the sadness, out of the grief, out of the confusion, out of the responsibility, and ultimately out of my life. I craved blessed nothingness, rest and reprieve. I almost got my wish.

I didn't tell Charles or my family what happened. From my weary viewpoint, I simply didn't want them to fuss and I certainly didn't want to take care of them as they worried about me. I had enough to be concerned about without dealing with their judgment, panic and anxiety. I simply limped through the pain and rarely sat down to rest. I hid my bruised body and smiled when I felt like crying.

From where I sit today, I see the foolishness of it all. Yet, in the midst of the experience I was numb and simply wanted to escape. I was bent to the point of breaking and I just wanted to snap. I was exhausted to the point of collapse and simply wanted rest. In this state of desperation, I didn't listen to myself with nearly fatal results. I acted tough and brave when perhaps the universe was teaching me to reach out for help. I was surrounded by support, yet I was determined to do it all alone. *Hello! Elizabeth? Welcome to your life!*

Buried deep in this event was the seed of a vital lesson just waiting to be uncovered. I was too busy playing super-woman to get the message. What else did I miss in my inability to surrender to support and fully receive all this chapter had to offer?

Chapter Seventeen

— ● —

THE POWER TO LOOSEN AND LIFT

"No person was ever honored for what they received.
Honor has been their reward for what they gave."
— Calvin Coolidge 1872-1933,
Former President of the United States

જ

Cancer has the ability to be a transformative event. At least that was my experience and Charles' experience as well. One of the many incredible blessings that we experienced during Charles' final months was a gentleness and lovingness that was unknowable before this time. Each touch, every word, kiss, caress, or gesture held within it a love and tenderness I can still feel today. It is born of devotion, unquestioning trust, and potent love.

Ironically, I think the most special times of our marriage occurred in his dying. His final weeks held such simplicity. There was no room for pettiness. No room for ego. No room for complication or angst. Life became simple in a way. It all came down to life and death. What a change from the complicated lives we brought together when we first met.

For three and one-half years I watched cancer transform Charles' body from a tall, heavy set, burly bear to a rail-thin, emaciated, shrunken shell of a man. Yet, as the weight and muscle fell away, I also watched as the disease transformed and polished his very soul until it shone like a radiant gem of priceless value. While his body became empty, his soul flourished.

Charles and I chose to face the experience of cancer full on. We embraced the journey and invited our family, friends and community to experience it as well. We chose to allow it to mold us, carry us, move us, shape us, and, at times, batter us.

Richard Bach, in his remarkable book *Illusions,* talks of a creature among creatures that lives life clinging to the bottom of a river. While this creature desires to experience the current found only in release, the others around it criticize it and speak of the certain death that will come from letting go. Yet, let go it did.

While the current battered the creature on the rocks for a short time, soon it was lifted free from the bottom and sailed with the current. When the others downstream saw the creature floating freely, they pointed and exclaimed that it was miraculous.

Charles let go and, despite being battered, he floated freely with the current of his life. He modeled what it means to choose happiness in the darkest of times. He chose to be grateful for everything. Absolutely everything! A touch, a glass of juice, a cold wash cloth on his brow, a cup of hot soup, a visit from a friend, or a hand to hold as he made his way to the bathroom. He chose gratitude not in an *"I'm-so-grateful-yet-undeserving"* way but from a place of fullness and a joy in communion of souls. He did this not just because he felt blessed, but to bless the giver. With dignity and grace at all times, he chose gratitude.

In August, just three months before his death, we hosted a marvelous party in Charles' honor. It was a good-bye party, the very essence of *"bittersweet"*. His entire family gathered from all over the country and so did countless friends. The party was complete when my three-year-old goddaughter, in a bright yellow dress, twirled in the sunshine beneath the apple tree as time stood still and all our guests looked on.

On this picture perfect summer day, we wanted to celebrate Charles in some special way. While a roast was suggested, our collective love for him would not allow us to ridicule or chide him in any way. Instead our celebration included a very *"gentle basting"*.

After a sumptuous potluck feast was devoured, we shared countless stories and memories, laughter and tears, as we encircled Charles in the shade as he sat on his lawn chair.

Those who attended the party initially felt this ritual of celebration would be our gift to Charles. Yet, in hindsight, I recognize the gift he gave to us. He allowed us to celebrate him. He received our love.

Charles was positively transformed by his journey with

cancer. While he was always a very physically attractive man, his inner beauty shone through him transforming his very being. He positively glowed from within. Charles' ever-present grace was revealed to us all in the opening of his life and his death.

So many who visited him in his final months felt that they received far more than they gave. This was his lifelong gift that cancer simply accentuated. Cancer loosened the grips of pride, the stifling weight of arrogance, the illusion of separateness and lifted him to a holy spot. He died beautifully and in his death all was transformed.

Chapter Eighteen

HAND WASH

"You will find as you look back upon your life that the moments when you have truly lived are the moments when you have done things in the spirit of love."
- Henry Drummond, 1851-1897,
Scientist, Evangelist, Author

ॐ

At the Fluff and Fold, I washed all my *"delicates"* in the large wash tub with gentle detergent, carefully wrapped them in a fluffy towel to remove as much water as possible, and laid them carefully out to dry. I was taught as a young child to treat my delicates with something approaching reverence. In a wash and wear, rough and tumble world, delicates were rare and often costly. As Charles' health declined, he too became more delicate. So did my emotional well being. All around him handled him with tender gentle care. I wished that someone, somewhere could do the same for my heart.

A few months before his death it became more and more challenging for Charles to perform the daily ritual of bathing. Getting out of bed, walking to the bathroom, undressing, climbing into the tub, washing up, drying off, dressing, returning to the bedroom and getting back in the bed took more energy than he could summon. As a result, I began to bathe him in bed. Charles' sister, Anne, an experienced nurse, graciously and thoroughly instructed me in the fine art of a sponge bath.

Since the beginning, I was keenly aware of Charles'

desire to make his own decisions and chart the course of his care. As a result, bathing him initially felt like such an insult, as though I was treating him like an infant incapable of tending to his own basic needs. Surprisingly enough, by the time it became necessary, my fiercely independent husband didn't object to this new daily ritual at all. He reveled in the attention and the intimacy of the process. In his gentle and loving way, he let me know that this was a good thing, that he welcomed the touch and intimacy and was grateful for my care. At first I was more uncomfortable with the process than he was.

As the weeks passed, I let go of my discomfort and allowed myself to experience the beauty of bathing my husband as the blessing that it was. I found it was one of the ways I could show him my love. It was a marvelous way for us to connect through physical touch. It provided me the experience of complete service from the most sincere place of devotion. It was a gift to us both and drew us even closer together in his final weeks.

One Sunday evening, five days before Charles passed away, my dearest friend, Deborah, came over to be with me. While Christopher stayed in the house with his dad, she and I walked out to the meadow off the front yard and watched a magnificent sunset. As the colors of approaching night decorated the sky, we sat silently holding hands on a bench and took it all in. A flock of Canadian geese flying in "V" formation made their way across the meadow and provided spectacular viewing for the two of us on our peaceful perch.

After a few short minutes, I felt drawn back to the house. As his father's health became increasingly unstable, I made an agreement with Christopher. I told him that at no time would he have to be solely responsible for his dad's care. The image of something happening to Charles while Christopher was alone in the house haunted my dreams. In my short time with Deborah, while only four hundred yards from the house, I had broken my agreement.

As we walked the short distance back to the house, Deborah and I both commented on how the spectacular colors and beauty of the sunset were so much like Charles in his final days. The most beautiful colors, the quietest peace, the promise of rest all came packaged in the end of that day. In the end of a life…

In his final weeks, Charles loved massages. Back at the house, I asked Deborah if she would mind helping give Charles a massage. His muscles were tight and sore from hours in bed, and the sensations of loving touch brought him great pleasure in his monotonous, drug induced, quiet days.

She readily agreed and within minutes, the bedroom was silent except for the sounds of our hands rubbing lotion on his shoulders, arms, hands, legs and feet. The light was soft and time stood still. Charles' smiles, when he was awake, expressed complete gratitude and appreciation, without guile or ego. He long ago released any unwillingness or inability to receive. He soaked it all in graciously and gratefully as his skin soaked in the lotion and his body received the tender care of our hands.

I'm not sure who received more that night. We were so very connected, the three of us, there in the dimly lit bedroom with so little sound. With his characteristic grace, Charles gave us a marvelous and rare gift. He allowed us to give fully to one who could unabashedly receive.

It was a perfect circle of giving and receiving. I received the understanding that one cannot exist without the other. Giving is incomplete without those to receive. Receiving is empty longing without those who graciously give. All these lessons were wrapped up in the simplest of acts.

In his final weeks, Charles and I experienced a universal wholeness and completeness that was so genuine and simple. So real and uncalculated. So authentic and fulfilling. The intensity of our love and the reality of our pain coexisted peacefully, yin and yang, like two perfect halves of an exquisite seashell.

Chapter Nineteen

━━━━●━━━━

AND THEN WE HAD PIE...

*"As a man in his last breath
drops all he is carrying, each breath is
a little death that makes us free."*
— Mark Nepo, author,
The Book of Awakening

ꙮ

Charles passed away on Thanksgiving Day. What a remarkable end to an incredibly abundant and richly blessed life. What a beautifully symbolic beginning to life's greatest adventure.

It was an unseasonably warm day in an unusually warm fall. Charles' family had finally headed home after many autumn visits and my family was yet to arrive for the feasting. Christopher had been with us for a few days and he was scheduled to leave later that morning for Thanksgiving with his mom.

I arose at 6:00 a.m. to put the turkey in the oven and found Charles alert, talkative and thirsty. His spunkiness, after so many days of *"spunklessness"*, was a bit surprising but I was too tired to really make much note of it.

He asked for some juice, which, when I brought it, he drank down in mere moments rather than with his regular labored sipping. This was most amazing as it had been days since he had eaten and his fluid intake had slowed considerably as well.

We talked for a bit in the pre-dawn darkness as I perched on his bed, his head inclined, gently holding hands. Today I'd give nearly anything to remember exactly what we said. It is so incredible that I can remember so many things in the finest detail yet his exact words elude me.

After a bit I said, *"I've really got to get a bit more sleep, honey. I'm pooped. I'm going to turn out the light and rest a bit more. We can chat more when I wake you at 8:00 a.m. for your meds. O.K.?"*

He was a bit reluctant. Did he sense his time was near? But he acquiesced and as I drifted off, four feet away, I knew he was still awake. I knew he was simply lying there listening to me breathe, taking in the quiet sounds of my much needed sleep.

Had I known it would be the last full conversation we would have, I would have surely stayed awake knowing rest would be plentiful another time. I often resist the urge to kick myself for not staying up to talk with him. Over the months and years, I'd missed countless hours of sleep. Why was I so insistent now? From where I stand today, this is yet another powerful reminder that we never really know what lies even a few minutes ahead of us. Yet another reminder to stay present and watchful, fully awake to the world and the wonders therein.

When I awoke later, it was a bit tougher to rouse him. I

gave him his meds then a long, leisurely sponge bath, a ritual he and I had grown to love and cherish. I massaged his shrunken, fragile arms and legs the way he loved. I rubbed lotion on his face, feet and hands, and also brushed his teeth. He lay quietly in his bed as I did all of this, a gentle smile on his face. Few words were exchanged.

As I tried to change his shirt, I asked him to help me by raising his hands. He made an attempt, then gave me a look of resignation. I assured him it was O.K. and I eased the shirt over his body and kissed his guileless face. His smile was so precious, a little embarrassed at his weakness, yet grateful for my assistance.

I left him at that point and went on about my day. Family was coming, Christopher would be up in a bit and his mom would be by to pick him up in just one hour. I showered, dressed, finished cleaning the house and generally puttered with Thanksgiving preparations.

I looked in on Charles every few minutes. He seemed to be getting weaker, more distant each time. By the time Cheryl and her husband, Ken, came to get Christopher, Charles was slipping. He was a bit agitated, unable to communicate, not able to engage.

We all stood silently in the bedroom around the bed, unsure of what to say. I held Charles and inquired of

Cheryl, in an overly bright manner, about their weekend plans. Then we all stood together in the quiet of the room. All present wept quietly, the only sound was Charles' labored breathing. I can't imagine how painful it was for them to say good-bye and leave.

After they left I called Charles' family but only reached his brother, John. We talked for a bit and I told him I felt Charles' time was near. I rigged up a phone to reach into the bedroom so John could talk to Charles. For seven minutes I held the phone to Charles' ear as I held him and John said his good-byes.

I can only imagine how it was for John, hearing only rapid, shallow breathing on the other end of the line, to speak words that would somehow capture their life together and bring it to a close. My heart broke for John, there in his Denver home miles from where he wanted to be as his brother slipped away.

Shortly after noon I entered the bedroom to find Charles in his final struggle. His arms were locked across his chest and he was fighting, unwilling to surrender. It appeared as though two angels were trying to lift him up so he could stand and take his leave. Charles, however, was not ready to go.

His straining noises in our otherwise silent house reached inside my chest and silently shattered my already battered heart. His strength was amazing. I was unable to calm him so I simply held him and stroked him instead. Finally, I curled up in the bed, wrapped him in my arms and tried to soothe him. Nothing seemed to work and Charles struggled on.

As 12:30 approached I knew my family would soon be arriving with Thanksgiving dinner fixings in tow, unaware of what was happening. I left Charles for only a minute to put a small note on the door inviting them in and to make themselves at home. In Cabalka fashion, they arrived right on time, a Thanksgiving feast in hand. I popped out to the living room to greet them and make them aware of what was happening.

A few minutes after my family's arrival, Charles calmed himself. It was amazing, like the calm after a giant summer storm. He simply let go and began to drift and float effortlessly in my arms. I stayed with him for the next two hours, holding him and soothing his hot forehead. Few words were spoken as I sat and gently held him .

My family came in and out of the bedroom as the next two hours passed. We looked at photos, shared memories, and sat quietly together. Some part of me knew that he was leaving. Yet another part, the one that had held him many dark nights when he had stopped breathing, saying good bye only to have him eat a three course meal the next day, that part of me couldn't really believe this was it. Yet I stayed with him, meanwhile encouraging my family to continue their meal preparations. Despite all this, we still needed to eat. And they needed something to do.

In hindsight, I think the angels came to take Charles a little after noon, two hours before he passed. I believe his struggle was his resistance to leaving just then. I believe he didn't want me to be alone when he left and that he used every ounce of remaining strength to hang on until my family arrived. That was his final act of love for me in this, his human life. He was thoughtful to the end. Scheduling events just so until his final human breath.

About 2:30, while my family ate their subdued Thanksgiving feast, I sat cradling my most beloved friend just down the hall. A small voice inside me said, *"Go, join your family. Eat. Be refreshed. Charles is in good hands"* I resisted for a while, but the gentle voice persisted.

Finally I leaned close to Charles' ear and said, *"I am going to join my family at the table for a little bit. If you need to go while I'm away, go ahead. I'll catch up with you another time. I love you my handsome husband, always and forever."*

I sat at the Thanksgiving table, not hungry, simply numb, trying to talk with my family and somehow make this less difficult for them. Where I found the strength to care for them and their frail emotional state is beyond me.

When I returned to the bedroom, twenty minutes later, I watched Charles' chest fall for the very last time. With my head to his chest I could hear no beating nor could I find a pulse. Gentle warm breath came from his mouth as his body let go and his soul departed.

My father came in and, not knowing what else to do, offered me his watch, which I had used many times that day to take Charles' pulse. I looked into my father's sad and concerned eyes and told him Charles was gone.

Looking into Charles' eyes confirmed my suspicions. At that moment I understood that Charles was not simply his body. He was so much more than that. When he was gone, that spark that made Charles unique was gone as well. He was free while his body remained.

I slowly left the bedroom and told my family Charles was gone. I sat heavily in my seat, dazed and unsure of what to do next.

After calls to the hospice nurse and the local funeral home, my mother, adorned in Thanksgiving apron, broke the still of the room.

"Would anyone like some pie?" she inquired apprehensively.

It's hard to adequately express how much I loved and appreciated my mother in that moment. Living always by the Methodist code *"When they're grievin', feed 'em"*, my mother would have made church theologians proud. Her desire to comfort us all in this most intensely awkward and distressing time was beautiful and deeply moving. Just a few moments before, my life could have shattered irreparably. Her simple question was my anchor to life, a reminder that it goes on.

Not knowing exactly what to say, we all looked at one another and said, *"Why yes, let's do."*

And so we had pie...

❦

Charles Martin Winger, age 43, began life's greatest adventure on Thanksgiving Day 2001. The struggle is over. Now, peace.

Charles was tremendously proud of his roots. His years at Kansas State University firmly cemented a life-long passion for all things purple. His career spanned a variety of occupations from Continental Grain and Hallmark Cards to Hennepin Ave United Methodist Church and Koinonia Retreat Center. While he loved to travel and watch football, his greatest joy in life was his son, Christopher, of whom he would always be fiercely proud.

Charles' unflinching belief in God and the life everlasting was his greatest comfort especially in his final moments. His ministry did not end when his mobility left him but continued in earnest with gentleness and grace. He gave everyone he touched the gift of seeing what it means to live life completely, to love unconditionally, and to serve all with an open, joyful heart. This was evident throughout his entire life, yet especially tangible in recent months.

His three and one-half year journey with cancer touched hundreds of lives around the world. He gently, yet repeatedly and unselfishly, shared his passionate message of healthful diet and lifestyle, prevention as the cure, the incredible power of the mind, positive thinking, and clean living through word, action, and deed. This message has touched and saved lives across the globe.

"Well done, good and faithful servant."

Coming Fall 2004...

The Ironies of Grief
Shall I laugh or shall I cry?

By Elizabeth Cabalka

Once again, Elizabeth perfectly captures her story and the stories of others. This book features stories of "grief moments" when a choice makes all the difference. Featuring the hilarious, ironic story: *"Sorry for your loss and please press one to leave a message."*

Reserve your copy today:
www.elizabethcabalka.com

Coming Fall 2005...

I Love You Too
Dating and loving again
after losing a spouse.

By Elizabeth Cabalka

*"Dating? You've got to be kidding.
Ugh. At nearly forty, dating was the last
thing I thought I would need to consider.
The truth was, however, I was lonely. I
wanted companionship and was tired of
being alone. So I took a deep breath,
closed my eyes, and hesitantly said
yes."*

So begins the third book in the
powerful and poignant series
by Elizabeth Cabalka.

Reserve your copy today:
www.elizabethcabalka.com

HIP *Healthy Insights Press*

Quick Order Form

email Orders: ecabalka@lakedalelink.net

Postal Orders: Healthy Insights
PO Box 438
Annandale, MN. 55302-0438

Please send the following **Wednesdays at the Fluff 'n' Fold:**

☐ Paperback version $14.95

☐ CD PDF version $12.95

☐ CD Audio version $19.95

*Orders of 10 or more items will receive a 20% discount off cover price.

Please send more FREE information on:

☐Future Books ☐ Speaking/Seminars ☐Mailing List ☐Consulting

Name:_____

Address:_____

City:_____ State:_____ Zip:_____

Telephone:_____

email address:_____

Sales Tax: Please add 6.5% for products shipped to Minnesota addresses.

Shipping by air:
U.S.: $4.00 for first book or disk and $2.00 for each additional product (estimate).
International: $9.00 for first book or disk; $5.00 for each additional product (estimate).

Payment Method:

☐ Check *(payable to Healthy Insights Press)* ☐ Credit Card

Card number:_____

Type:_____

Name on card_____

Exp. date:_____

www.elizabethcabalka.com